To Howard Russell
Trust everyone — but always cut the cards. Tombstone, A.T.
6/10/06
Ben T. Traywick

FRAIL PRISONERS
in YUMA TERRITORIAL PRISON

edited by **BEN T. TRAYWICK**

Published by
Red Marie's Bookstore
P.O. Box 891
Tombstone, Arizona

Acknowledgement

Most of the information and photographs used in this publication were supplied by the Yuma Territorial Prison State Park. The author is most grateful to Josephine Masterson and the staff at this park, for their co-operation, patience, and understanding.

Ben T. Traywick

Frail Prisoners
in Yuma Territorial Prison

Edited by
Ben T. Traywick

Published by Red Marie's 1997

Copyright by Ben T. Traywick 1997

Table of Contents

Chapter	Name	Crime	Page
1.	Lizzie Gallagher	Manslaughter	1
2.	May Woodman	Manslaughter	9
3.	Allegracia de Otero	Liquor to Indians	17
4.	Manuela Fimbres	Murder	19
5.	Jennie McCleary	Aggravated Assault	27
6.	Georgie Clifford	Manslaughter	33
7.	Isabelle Washington	Manslaughter	51
8.	Susie Smith	Stolen Goods	55
9.	Teresa Garcia	Stolen Goods	59
10.	Maria Moreno	Manslaughter	67
11.	Trinidad Montano	Burglary	75
12.	Exie Sedgmore	Assault Deadly Weapon	81
13.	Pearl Hart	Robbery	97
14.	Elena Estrada	Manslaughter	109
15.	Alfrida Mercer	Adultery	115
16.	Rosa Duran	Grand Larceny	121
17.	Bertha Trimble	Rape	125
18.	Jesus Chacon	Arson	131
19.	Kate Nelson	Adultery	133
20.	Pearl Eiker	Manslaughter	143
21.	Francisca Robles	Assault Deadly Weapon	149
22.	Saferina Garcia	Felony	155
23.	Ada Parks	Grand Larceny	157
24.	Pinkie Dean	Assault Deadly Weapon	165
25.	Angelita Berdusco	Adultery	169
26.	Eulogia Bracamonte	Assault Deadly Weapon	177
27.	Angelita Sonoqui	Adultery	183
28.	E.M. Bridgeford	Grand Larceny	191
29.	Fannie King	Manslaughter	193

29

women served time at Yuma Territorial Prison

Their crimes were:

Manslaughter	8
Murder	1
Aggravated assault	1
Selling liquor to Indians	1
Receiving stolen goods	2
Burglary	1
Assault with a deadly weapon	4
Robbery	1
Adultery	4
Grand larceny	3
Rape	1
Arson	1
Felony	1

Average prison sentence . . . . 2 years, 4 months
Average sentence served . . . . 12.76 months
Average of prisoners' age . . . . 26.31 years
Age - oldest prisoner . . . . 55 years
Age - youngest prisoner . . . . 16 years

Author's Introduction

On the morning of July 1, 1876, a line of men toiled up the hill to the sun blasted walls of the Territorial Prison at Yuma to enter this new prison that they had built themselves on the 8.38 acres that the town of Yuma had deeded to the Territory of Arizona for the penitentiary.

This prison was to endure for 34 years--1876 until its abandonment in 1909. During this time period 3,069 prisoners passed thru its walls. Of this total number, 29 were women--referred to as frail prisoners.

Yuma Territorial Prison was one of the first projects attempted by the Territorial government. Money was hard to obtain as the entire Territory of Arizona had less than 50,000 people. The City of Yuma contained only a few hundred.

In the beginning, the 1868 Fifth Legislative Assembly passed a bill to locate the Territorial Prison near Phoenix. Nothing was done toward construction however. During the Eighth Territorial Legislature in 1876 Granville Oury introduced a bill that eventually created a bond issue to allow construction of the penitentiary that had been authorized by the 1868 Legislature.

Jose Maria Redondo and Representative R.B. Kelly of Yuma County submitted a bit of political chicanery by eliminating Phoenix from the bill and substituting Yuma.

Rocks for the prison's foundation were taken from the prison quarry. In this foundation alone 60,000 pounds of lime were used as were 51,000 cubic feet of rock.

At one time, 21 foreign countries were represented by the inmates. The most predominant nationality was Mexican which numbered more than half consistently. The census of 1890 revealed that the prison contained 11 Germans, 8 Scots and Welch, 29 Irish, 10 English, 1 Russian, 1 Norwegian, and 20 Chinese as well as the usual number of Mexican and Indians.

Less than 1% of the total number of prisoners were women. However, this small number of females garnered more publicity and caused more problems than all the men. Every superintendent said that they were a terrible nuisance. Many women were pardoned or paroled just to get rid of them.

Myth-makers would have the reader believe that no one ever escaped from this stone fortress. It is true that no prisoner ever escaped from the inside prison walls or from a locked cell. Twenty-six inmates did make successful escapes--eight others were shot to death in escape attempts.

The Quechan Indians lived near the prison and knew the desert and its ways better than most. When a prisoner escaped they were most happy to take their trail, anxious to earn the $50 in gold that was paid for the prisoner's return--dead or alive. Some trackers killed their quarry at the first opportunity as a dead prisoner could present no danger to the captor. Some did not, as live ones did not smell so bad and did not have to be carried.

One hundred and twelve prisoners died during their period of confinement--most deaths caused by tuberculosis.

No executions were carried out on the prison grounds as legal executions were the responsibility of county governments.

Paroles and pardons appeared to be easy to obtain during those times and most offenders served only small fractions of their sentences.

William Mall was the first prisoner at the Territorial Prison and, as such, he was given the dubious honor of being No. 1. Mall had been sentenced to life for the crime of second degree murder. He had begun serving his time in the Yuma County Jail on May 20, 1875. When the new prison on the hill was ready for prisoners he was transferred there July 1, 1876.

A man named C. Jackson, from Gila County was the last prisoner sent to Yuma. As such, he was identified as No. 3069.

By 1907, the prison on the hill was overcrowded and no land room was available for expansion. It was decided that a new facility would be constructed at Florence. To perform this construction, 18 longtime prisoners were taken from Yuma to the new site. Other convicts were slowly added until they numbered 140. Less trustworthy inmates and the female prisoners were left at Yuma during construction. The last prisoner left Yuma on September 15, 1909. They were handcuffed and transported to Florence by train.

Three women, Pinkie Dean, E.M. Bridgeford, and Fannie King were still inmates at Yuma. They were also transferred to Florence.

When the last person left the Yuma Territorial Prison, it, as provided for in the deed, once again became the property of the city of Yuma.

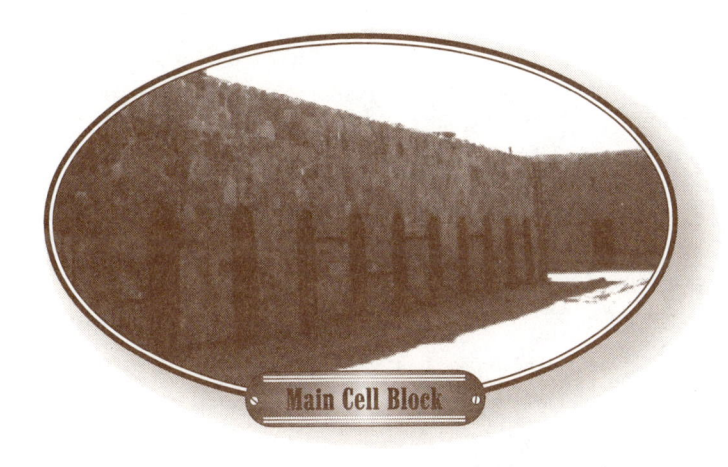

Chapter 1

Lizzie Gallagher ~No. 26

On May 24, 1878, James Moriarty, Private, Co. G, Sixth Cavalry, lately from Fort Grant, was stabbed in the heart and killed. Lizzie Gallagher was arrested on suspicion of having struck the fatal blow.

It appears that a man, named Frank Jones, had been conducting a variety show in Yuma. When the show ended he then provided a dance and monte games as further entertainment.

While at the dance on that fateful night, Lizzie had been insulted by Private Moriarty. In a fit of anger, she grabbed up a knife and stabbed him, the blade severing his heart.

An examination was held by Justice Brinley on May 25, 1878. The evidence was produced as were several witnesses to the incident. The murder weapon was produced by the county sheriff. It was determined by the Justice that there was enough evidence to cause Lizzie to be held for action by the Grand Jury.

On November 9, 1878, the Grand Jury indicted Lizzie Gallagher for murder. On November 11, 1878, she was arraigned on the indictment. Her date for her indictment plea was set.

Lizzie, in open court with her counsel, pled that she was not guilty of the offense charged in the indictment. In the next session of her trial, her counsel Messrs. Rowell and Purdy, had her request that she be allowed by the court to withdraw her plea of not guilty of the offense charged and to be allowed to plead guilty of the offense of manslaughter.

The court then instructed the defendant as to the effect of such plea and of the punishment that was provided by statue for the crime of manslaughter. There was no objection made by District Attorney H.N. Alexander. Lizzie was allowed to plead guilty of the offense of manslaughter and such was entered into the records of the court.

Lizzie Gallagher was sentenced by the court on November 16, 1878. At that time, the court informed her of the nature of the indictment against her for murder, her plea of not guilty to that charge, the court allowing her to withdraw that plea and her plea of guilty of manslaughter. The court then had instructed her as to the effect of such a plea.

The defendant was then asked if she had any legal cause to show why judgment should not be pronounced against her; to which question she replied that she had none. Since there was no sufficient cause being shown or appearing to the court, judgment was rendered.

"That whereas, the said Lizzie Gallagher, having in this court pled that she is guilty of the offense of manslaughter--it is therefore ordered, adjudged, and decreed, that the said Lizzie Gallagher be punished by imprisonment at hard labor in the Territorial Prison of the Territory of Arizona, for the term of one year and three months. You, the said defendant, are remanded into the custody of the sheriff of the County of Yuma, to be by him delivered into the custody of the proper officers of said Territorial Prison."

Lizzie was delivered to the Territorial Prison on November 17, 1879, and was immediately returned to the county jail for "safekeeping." It is difficult to imagine the turmoil caused by the injection of one female into a horde of men locked away from the rest of the world and female companionship. And into such an environment that had no accommodations for keeping this female segregated.

Meanwhile, Lizzie had a friend, named Brown who did a travelling saloon business along the railroad being built, supplying the workers with liquor and other entertainment. Brown heard about Lizzie's jail sentence and soon appeared in Yuma.

Brown married Lizzie and then began a program to obtain her release. It must be that he had some political influence or it is possible that Lizzie was just too much of a "problem" for political and prison officials.

For some reason Lizzie was removed from the county jail and delivered to the Territorial Prison on October 1, 1879.

The Territorial Papers reveal the following document:

Territory of Arizona
Executive Department

To all to whom these presents shall come Greeting. Whereas it has been made known to me that Lizzie Gallagher was arraigned before the District Court of the Second Judicial District in November, 1878 upon the charge of murder and was upon the admission of her plea of guilty of manslaughter sentenced to fifteen months imprisonment in the Territorial Prison. And whereas, a petition has been presented to me signed generally by the good and responsible citizens of Yuma, asking the remission of her further punishment upon satisfactory grounds and on account also of her youth and good conduct during solitary confinement.

Now, therefore, for the reasons above given and because her pardon is strongly urged by the Judge before whom she was tried, I, John C. Fremont, Governor of the Territory of Arizona, do hereby grant full pardon to the said Lizzie Gallagher and direct that she be set at liberty.

Given under my hand and the seal of the Territory of Arizona this 22nd day of November, 1879.

J.C. Fremont
Governor
John J. Gosper
Secretary of Territory
By J.E. Anderson
Asst. Secretary of Territory

Lizzie Gallagher Brown departed Yuma with her new husband and followed the railroad camps still conducting the "travelling saloon" toward Tucson.

She was an unknown, who came from nowhere, who killed James Moriarty, was arrested, tried, and sentenced to the Territorial Prison, married, pardoned, and disappeared into oblivion--all in less than two years. Her only claim to fame was that she was the first woman sentenced to Yuma.

Court Record of Lizzie Gallagher

Thereupon the trial of the above entitled action set for Monday Nov. 18th, 1878 at ten o'clock a.m.

Friday, November 15th, 1878

The Territory of Arizona)
    against   ) Indictment for Murder
Lizzie Gallagher   )

Now comes into open Court H.N. Alexander Esq. District Attorney, and the above named defendant Lizzie Gallagher, with her counsel, Messrs. Rowell and Purdy. Whereupon the defendant, by her counsel, with the consent of the attorney for the prosecution, asks leave of the Court to withdraw her plea heretofore entered of "Not Guilty" of the offense charged in the indictment herein and to be allowed to plead guilty of the offense of manslaughter.

The defendant having been instructed by the Court as to the effect of such plea and of the penalties provided by statute for the crime of manslaughter, and no objection being made by the District Attorney then and there present in open Court, the said defendant Lizzie Gallagher pleads that she is guilty of the offense of manslaughter, which said pleas is ordered by the Court to be herein entered of record.

It was thereupon ordered that the said defendant be and appear before this Court for sentence tomorrow morning at ten o'clock. Thereupon the Court adjourned until tomorrow morning November 16th, 1878 at ten o'clock.

DeForest Porter
Judge.

Saturday, November 16th, 1878

At ten o'clock a.m. of this day the Court met pursuant to adjournment. Present: Hon. DeForest Porter, Judge, Sheriff, District Attorney and Clerk.

The Territory of Arizona)
    vs.   )   Sentence
Lizzie Gallagher)

The time set for passing sentence upon the above named defendant,
Lizzie Gallagher, having arrived. The District Attorney with the said defendant and her counsel, Messrs. Rowell and Purdy came into Court. The defendant was duly informed by the Court of the nature of the indictment found against her for the crime of murder, committed the twenty fourth day of May A.D. 1878; of her arraignment and plea of "not guilty as charged in said indictment;" of her having, by leave of this Court, withdrawn her said plea of "Not Guilty" of the offense charged in said indictment; and of her plea that "the defendant pleads that she is guilty of the offense of manslaughter," after having been instructed by the Court as to the effect of such plea. The defendant was then asked if she had any legal cause to show why judgment should not be pronounced against her, to which she replied that she had none. And no sufficient cause being shown or appearing to the Court thereupon the Court renders its judgment: That whereas, the said Lizzie Gallagher, having in this Court plead that she is guilty of the offense of manslaughter - It is therefore ordered, adjudged and decreed, that the said Lizzie Gallagher be punished by imprisonment at hard labor in the Territorial Prison of the Territory of Arizona, for the term of one year and three months. You, the said defendant, are remanded into the custody of the sheriff of the County of Yuma, to be by him delivered into the custody of the proper officers of said Territorial Prison.

ꙮ Frail Prisoners in Yuma Territorial Prison ꙮ

TERRITORIAL PRISON AT YUMA, A.T.

Description of Convict

NAME:
   Lizzie Gallagher
ALIAS:

CRIME:
   Manslaughter
COUNTY:
   Yuma
LEGITIMATE OCCUPATION:

HABITS:

OPIUM:

HEIGHT:
   5' 1"
SIZE OF HEAD:

COLOR EYES:
   Gray
MARRIED:
CAN READ:
:
WHERE EDUCATED:

NUMBER:
   26
SENTENCE:
   1 yr., 3 mos. from 11/11/1878
NATIVITY:
   Irish
AGE:
   20
TOBACCO:

RELIGION:

SIZE FOOT:

WEIGHT:

COLOR HAIR:
   Brown
CHILDREN:

CAN WRITE:
FORMER IMPRISONMENT

NEAREST RELATIVE:

WHEN AND HOW DISCHARGED:
   Pardoned by Governor Fremont, November 26, 1879.

PRISON RECORD

- Taken from the Prison Diary:
- Taken to the prison Nov. 17, 1878, returned to county jail for safe keeping.
- Oct. 1, 1879 - Removed from County jail to prison.
- Nov. 26, Pardoned Nov. 26, 1879.
- *No photo available.*

~ Lizzie Gallagher ~

Frail Prisoners

Women in Yuma
(l. to r.) Elena Estrada, Pearl Hart, & Rosa Duran

❦ Frail Prisoners in Yuma Territorial Prison ❦

Cell Block Entrance

Chapter 2

May Woodman ~ No. 168

About 10:30 a.m. on February 23, 1883, William Kinsman was standing in front of the Oriental Saloon on Tombstone's Allen Street. Here, he was accosted by a very angry woman. After a few choice words she pulled a .38 caliber revolver and shot him point blank.

The ball entered Kinsman's left side about four inches below the nipple and passed horizontally thru his body. The determined woman attempted to fire a second shot into the prone body of her victim, but the weapon was struck down by Chief of Police Coyle, the ball entering the sidewalk.

When the woman was arrested by Chief Coyle, she claimed to have been driven to the act by abuse received from Kinsman with whom she had been living for some months. After her arrival at City Hall, she asked Constable Ike Roberts if her shots had hit Kinsman. Upon being informed that she had not only hit him, but probably had killed him, she seemed quite happy to receive that news.

Kinsman lived about four hours after being shot. This young man was about twenty-five years old and had lived for a time in Virginia City. People in Tombstone knew him as a sporting man.

The dark haired, fair skinned woman was twenty-seven years old, went by the name of Mrs. May Woodman, and had arrived in Tombstone from Bodie some two years before. Jealousy was thought to be the reason she shot Kinsman.

Most likely it was a practical joker that caused this death. Someone placed an ad in the Tombstone Epitaph stating that William Kinsman had intentions of marrying May Woodman.

Frail Prisoners in Yuma Territorial Prison

Kinsman placed an article in the next issue that he had no intentions of committing matrimony with May, now or ever. Most likely when the woman read that public rejection she deliberately set out to kill Kinsman.

During her trial, May testified that she had shot Kinsman in self-defense. Evidently, no one believed her testimony as the Arizona Sentinel, May 19, 1883, reported:

"The jury in the case of the Territory vs. May Woodman, charged with the murder of Kinsman in Tombstone, returned a verdict of guilty of manslaughter."

Before May was sentenced, she attempted suicide by taking chloral hydrate and morphine. Dr. Goodfellow was summoned in time to save her life. The explanation as to how she had procured this poison was:

"For some days a mixture of chloral hydrate and morphine had been administered to May to produce sleep. This medicine, instead of taking when administered by her attendants, she carefully saved until quite a quantity of the deadly drug had accumulated."

Some explanation - not very acceptable - but.... Dr. Goodfellow discovered something else not known about May. His medical report stated that it was apparent that Kinsman or someone had beaten her severely even though she was pregnant. There had been no mention of these facts at her trial. May miscarried while in jail, and Dr. Goodfellow said that the fetus was at four or five months.

Most of the Tombstone public took sides against May in the shooting. Even the Epitaph printed a brief line to that effect. It read:

"It is said that May Woodman, who is confined in the county jail awaiting trial for murder is insane. The conclusion has been arrived at from her recent actions."

Judge Pinney overruled the motion for a new trial for May Woodman, convicted of manslaughter in killing Billy Kinsman last February, and sentenced her for five years in the penitentiary. Upon receiving the sentence she turned angrily to the Judge and remarked, "May God curse you forever!"

~ May Woodman ~

The Arizona Weekly Citizen, May 26, 1883, stated:
"The Full Penalty:

Judge Pinney, in sentencing May Woodman, who murdered Kinsman, in Tombstone, made use of the following language, which foreshadows a determination to mete out exact justice to criminals and stamp out crime by visiting the extreme penalties prescribed by law. The judge proceeded to state that, having been found guilty, it became his duty to pass sentence; that while his sympathy, as well as that of the community went out to her, being a woman, his duty as a magistrate prevented him from allowing it to warp his judgement, or stand in the way of justice. The custom so prevalent in this country of using weapons on slight pretext for the purpose of redressing wrongs especially at night, was commented on and condemned in the severest terms. The Judge, in conclusion, informed the prisoner that her term in the penitentiary could be utilized by her in preparation for a higher and better life. That the full limit of the law was comparatively light sentence taken in connection with her crime, and he felt that his duty compelled him to sentence the prisoner for the term of five years, the utmost limit prescribed for this offense."

Not long after May arrived at the Territorial Prison in Yuma she became the center of another controversy. She was pregnant again. All the prison officials maintained that it was absolutely impossible for any male to gain access to the women's portion of the prison. Whatever was said or done, the story was that the woman was pregnant and she certainly had not accomplished this feat all alone.

On November 24, 1883, an Arizona Sentinel reporter wrote with some sarcasm:

"If current reports be true a scandal of some magnitude will be made public in connection with the territorial prison administration, the irrepressible May Woodman from Tombstone notoriety having become with child since her incarceration in that secluded retreat on the Colorado."

The Sentinel later reported:
"To ascertain the truth or falsehood of the statement

made, (concerning May Woodman's pregnancy), a representative of the Sentinel visited the prison, and interviewed the prison authorities. Aside from the emphatic denial of the superintendent, the warden and the woman herself, we are convinced that under the circumstances such a condition of affairs would be impossible. The woman is kept under as strict discipline as the rest of the prisoners, occupies a cell which is inaccessible from others, and the key of her cell, after locking up at night, is deposited in a safe to which no one has access except the turn key. Of course, this report was started simply to injure Captain Ingalls, the superintendent of the prison, and has no foundation except in the imagination of some brute to whom a pure thought is an absolute stranger."

Whether the accusations were true or false, acting Arizona Governor Van Arman was so dismayed that he took action that was described in the Arizona Weekly Citizen, January 5, 1884: "May Woodman's Pardon"

Concerning the report in the Tombstone Epitaph that May Woodman had been pardoned, the records in the governor's office were examined this morning, and the fact was ascertained that Acting Governor Van Arman had granted her a conditional pardon, to take effect on the 16th (actually 15th) day of March, on condition that she leave the Territory and continue to reside beyond the limits of Arizona. The pardon was granted on the recommendation of all the court officers and about 200 prominent citizens of Tombstone, and no remonstrance against the granting of the pardon was presented. The effect of the pardon is to forever remove May Woodman from this Territory, and if she is found here after leaving, any sheriff or officer may return her and she will have to serve out the remainder of her term.

May Woodman accepted these terms and was pardoned. She took the first train to California and ... disappeared."

May Woodman

FUNERAL NOTICE

1883. *Tombstone A.T.*

FUNERAL NOTICE.

Tombstone A T

THE FUNERAL OF

William Kinsman,

Deceased, will take place on Sunday, February 25th, at 1 o'clock p. m., from the residence of his parents, corner of Seventh and Toughnut streets.

Friends and acquaintances are invited to attend.

Killed by May Woodman

William Kinsman

Letters for Pardon

May Woodman

Territory of Arizona
Executive DepartmentOffice of the Governor

    Whereas at the May term A.D. 1883 of the District Court in and for the County of Cochise, Arizona Territory, one May Woodman was tried and convicted of the Crime of Manslaughter and was by his Honor Judge Pinney sentenced to serve a term of five years in the Territorial Prison at Yuma, and whereas it has been represented to me by petition, signed by about 200 citizens of Tombstone, that the ends of Justice have been fully served by her imprisonment of three months in the Penitentiary. And whereas these same citizens earnestly pray for the release of said May Woodman from the Territorial Prison, and whereas I am of the opinion that the said May Woodman has not been sufficiently punished and should not at this time be released from the Territorial Prison. And whereas I do desire to protect society from the frenzy of a woman who it is contended was insane at the time, and who may possible get in the same mental condition again, and whereas I deem it improper that she should again reside in Tombstone or within the Territory of Arizona. NowMay Woodman therefore I, H.M. Van Arman, Acting Governor of Arizona Territory by virtue of the power vested in me, do grant a conditional pardon to the said May Woodman, said pardon to take effect on the 15th day of March A.D., 1884 on condition that she immediately go beyond the limits of this Territory and continue to reside without the limits of the Territory of Arizona done at Prescott the Capitol this 22nd day of August A.D, 1883.

> In witness whereof I have hereunto set my hand and caused the Great Seal of the Territory of Arizona to be fixed thereto.
> H.M. Van Arman
> Acting Governor

Attest:
    John S. Furnas
    Asst. Secty. Of the Territory

May Woodman having had read the condition of the within pardon accepted and agreed to the same in presence of witnesses.

                        Signed,
                        May Woodman

May Woodman

To the Secretary of Arizona Territory:

In compliance with Section 21 of Chapter 13 in regard to pardon, I make the following report in compliance with the within pardon I released May Woodman the person named in same on the fifteenth day of March A.D. 1884.

Dated: Yuma A.A.
March 15th, 1884

F.S. Ingalls,
Superintendent

Prison Cemetery

Frail Prisoners in Yuma Territorial Prison

TERRITORIAL PRISON AT YUMA, A.T.

Description of Convict

NAME:
   May Woodmn
ALIAS:

CRIME:
   Manslaughter
COUNTY:
   Cochise
LEGITIMATE OCCUPATION:
HABITS:

OPIUM:

HEIGHT:
   5' 4"
SIZE OF HEAD:

COLOR EYES:
   Gray
MARRIED:
CAN READ:
   Yes (Limited)
WHERE EDUCATED:

NUMBER:
   168
SENTENCE:
   5 years from
   5/30/1883

NATIVITY:
   American
AGE:
   27
TOBACCO:
RELIGION:

SIZE FOOT:

WEIGHT:

COLOR HAIR:
   Brown
CHILDREN:

CAN WRITE:
FORMER IMPRISONMENT:

NEAREST RELATIVE:

WHEN AND HOW DISCHARGED:
Pardoned by Govenor Tritle, March 15, 1884

PRISON RECORD

Taken from the Prison Diary:
- *Recieved at prison - June 8, 1883*
- *Pardoned March 15, 1884 by Act. Governor Van Arman on conditions*
- *Complexion: fair*

Chapter 3

Allegracia de Otero~No. 401

Allegracia was the oldest woman (55) ever sentenced to Yuma Territorial Prison. She was charged with selling liquor to Indians on two separate occasions.

She was charged in the court indictment of selling spirituous liquor to an Indian under the charge of an Indian agent. Specifically she sold one package of spirituous liquor containing one half gallon to Sa-mi-a-cup, an Indian, who belonged to the Pima Indian tribe and was under the charge of Indian Agent, Roswell G. Wheeler.

Pleading not guilty to the charge, Allegracia was provided Charles Kresham, a Spanish interpreter, and Sa-ma-he, an Indian interpreter. The trial then proceeded and she was found guilty by the jury.

She was ordered imprisoned in the Territorial Prison at Yuma for the term of 30 days and to pay a fine of $5.00.

As she was arrested for two counts of the same crime, she was also tried for selling one package of spirituous liquor to wit-one canteen full of whiskey, containing about one half gallon to "Kisto," a Pima Indian.

This time she pled guilty and after it was explained to her that it would be the duty of the court to impose on her the penalty required by law for the offense committed, only sentencing remained. Again, she was sentenced to the Territorial Prison at Yuma for 30 days and fined $5.00.

Allegracia served her time in Yuma and paid her fine, but the records do not show whether she returned to her profession as bootlegger. If she did, she was careful enough not to get caught again.

❦ Frail Prisoners in Yuma Territorial Prison ❦

TERRITORIAL PRISON AT YUMA, A.T.

Description of Convict

NAME:
  Allegracia de Otero
ALIAS:

NUMBER:
  401
SENTENCE:
  30 Days each charge
  $5.00 fine each charge
  10/18/86

CRIME:
  Selling liquor to Indians
  2 separate charges
COUNTY:
  Cochise
LEGITIMATE OCCUPATION:
HABITS:

NATIVITY:
  Mexican

AGE:
  27
TOBACCO:
RELIGION:

OPIUM:

SIZE FOOT:

HEIGHT:
SIZE OF HEAD:

WEIGHT:
COLOR HAIR:
  Black

COLOR EYES:
  Brown
MARRIED:

CHILDREN:

CAN WRITE:
  Yes

CAN READ:
  Yes
WHERE EDUCATED:
WHEN AND HOW DISCHARGED:
Expiration of sentence December 17, 1886

FORMER IMPRISONMENT:

NEAREST RELATIVE:

PRISON RECORD

Arizona Sentinel - October 23, 1886
Altagracia de Otero, and aged woman, was brought to the Territorial Prison on Tuesday by Deputy U.S. Marshall Underwood from Tucson to serve sixty days for selling whiskey to the Indians.
- Complexion: fair

Chapter 4

Manuela Fimbres~No. 572

The Tombstone Epitaph, December 28, 1888, carried the following report:

"Deputy Sheriff James Speedy of Nogales arrested at that place Juan Enriquez, the confessed murderer of Ah Foy, alias Sullivan of Tucson. It appears that he and two women decoyed the Chinaman to where he was killed when he struck him on the back of the head with a rock and broke his skull and then went to work on him with his knife. Jealousy was the cause.

Manuela Fimbres was identified as one of the women guilty of murdering the wealthy Chinaman. Although the newspaper cited jealousy as the cause, it is more likely that robbery was the motive. Enriquez disappeared into Sonora, but was captured after a short period of time.

Enriquez and Manuela were tried and convicted of Ah Foy's murder. The former was sentenced to 30 years in the Yuma Territorial Prison and the latter to 15 years. They were delivered to the prison by Sheriff Shaw on March 30, 1889, and began their sentences.

Locked up in prison did not entirely remove Manuela from the public eye. When she first arrived at Yuma she was carefully segregated from the other convicts and prison personnel. Superintendent Ingalls was succeeded by John H. Behan, who unwisely gave Manuela the run of the prison." Some writers report that she had two children in rapid succession. This writer finds evidence of only one.

Copies of the letter concerning Manuela from the Catholic priest to the governor and the governor's reply follow:

⚘ Frail Prisoners in Yuma Territorial Prison ⚘

The Arizona Sentinel, November 2, 1889, reported on Manuela:

"Manuela Fimbres, the Tucson woman convicted of being an accessory to the murder of a Chinaman last Spring and sentenced to 15 years imprisonment in the Territorial Prison gave birth to a baby boy last Monday. She has been an inmate of the penitentiary since March 28."

Author's note: Manuela was delivered to Yuma on March 30. Date of birth of the baby was October 26. She may have been pregnant when delivered to the prison.

Manuela made the Sentinel again on March 22, 1890:

"Manuela Fimbres, the woman serving a sentence of 15 years imprisonment in the Territorial Prison, is laying at the point of death from blood poisoning brought on by an attack of erysipelas. (sic) The woman was convicted one year ago in Pima County of being an accessory to the murder of a Chinaman killed in Tucson."

She also made the Moberly Monitor, Missouri, April 12, 1890: (excerpt)

"We must not forget to mention in this prison a six week's old infant, the mother of whom is a Mexican woman, who was incarcerated for the killing of a Chinaman. This woman is lying at the point of death, not withstanding all this, the little babe is doing well, and both mother and infant are receiving all attention possible. The Governor should pardon the woman before death claims her as its own."

On August 15, 1891, the Arizona Sentinel made a plea on behalf of little Luis Fimbrez:

"Many of our readers are aware of the fact that there is in the prison a little boy, Luis W. Fimbrez, a son of Maria Fimbrez, a prisoner sentenced for 15 years. The boy was born in the prison and is about two years old, and just the age when he should be put into a different school from that which he is now attending. The child is not to blame for his mother's crimes. He probably does not know, and never will, who his father was. The child is not to blame for this, nor for his father's crimes, even if he was guilty of any. To keep this child in prison, to educate him in the air of prison life, and subject him to the influences which pervade every avenue in which he circulates, is unkind, unjust, a blot upon our boasted civilization, and a disgrace to the times in which we live. Let the boy be taken out of that 'pen' and put into some institution where he will be educated for usefulness, and not for a criminal career in life."

In writing her conditional pardon, Governor N.O. Murphy stressed the facts that it required two guards to constantly watch over her and that she upset prison discipline.

Following her pardon, the Arizona Sentinel carried a final article on October 3, 1891:

"Manuela Fimbres, the only female convict in the Territorial Prison, was pardoned by the Governor and discharged last Friday. She was provided with plenty of comfortable clothing and sent to Tucson, where the Sheriff of Pima County sent her on to Mexico. Superintendent McInernay paid out a round sum of his own money for the woman, as the amount allowed by the Territory to a discharged convict was not enough for her needs. The Superintendent's kind and estimable wife very thoughtfully prepared a large basket of eatables amply sufficient for a journey of one week's duration."

Letter written on behalf of Manuela Fimbres by the Catholic Priest.

Yuma, Arizona
August 8th, 1889

HIS EXCELLENCY, L. WOLFLEY
Governor of Arizona
Phoenix, A.T.

Sir:
    Relying on the kindness which distinguishes your Excellency, I most respectfully recur to your clemency to-day.

Frail Prisoners in Yuma Territorial Prison

There is at the penitentiary a woman called, Manuela Fimbres, sentenced in Tucson about five months ago, for fifteen years; she is sick, and in a few weeks will be a mother. The penitentiary is not fit at all for a woman in her sad and delicate condition, for which all matrons have always shown regard.

Let, therefore, humanity and compassion influence you to use that power of pardoning given you by the law for such cases, or at least be kind as to see that she be sent to a house of refuge.

Hoping, Sir, that my request will meet with our kind consideration.

I remain very respectfully yours
Rev. F.B. Geniesse
Catholic Priest, attending the
        penitentiary.

Reply of the Governor:

Office of the Governor   Territory of Arizona
                                            Executive Department
Phoenix, Arizona, August 18th, 1889

Rev. J.B. Geniesse
Yuma, Arizona

Reverend Sir:

I have the honor to acknowledge the receipt of your esteemed favor, of August 8th, and to say that I have given the subject very careful consideration and very much thought.

Having been in Tucson for some little time I improved the opportunity thus afforded, to make diligent inquiry, concerning the merits of this woman, for whom you intercede, and permits me to say, that I really hoped to find some evidence, some extenuating circumstances, that would seem to in some degree at least authorize me to take the necessary steps to set this

~ Manuela Fimbres ~

woman free; but I regret to say the results of any investigation do not justify me in yielding to my sympathetic desire.

I presume your esteemed communication states all you can present to aid me in extending to her an act of mercy.

Her unfortunate condition is indeed to be lamented and I have weighted it carefully, but I am convinced as a result of inquiry that she merits the sentence imposed, and the good of our Territory demands that she suffer the penalty inflicted.

I see no reason for me to yield to the voice of sympathy in her case; I wish it were otherwise. It is often-times hundred-fold more easy to be merciful than to be just.

Her sad condition is indeed to be regretted. The Prison authorities, I trust, will, however, do all in their power to contribute to her comfort during her sickness, a duty imposed upon them both as citizens and as officers. Thanking you for your kind offices.

> I am Reverend Sir
> Very respectfully,
> Louis Wolfley, Governor

PROCLAMATION   **TERRITORY OF ARIZONA**

Granting Conditional Pardon   EXECUTIVE DEPARTMENT
   to
   M.Fimbrez

TO ALL TO WHOM THESE PRESENTS SHALL COME, GREETINGS

Whereas, I am informative of M. Fimbres, a female convict in the Territorial Prison at Yuma, who was convicted of the crime ofmurder at the March term of the District Court of the First Judicial District in and for Pima County, in the year 1889, and who was sentenced to a term of 15 years, is a constant source of care and anxiety on the management and demoralizing to discipline, and
Whereas, it is stated by the Prison authorities and other reputable citizens of this Territory, that her mental faculties are of the lowest order, and of common morality and decency she knows nothing; that the presence of this woman has a most demoralizing effect on prison discipline, and requires the almost constant attention of two guards to watch her, and

~ Frail Prisoners in Yuma Territorial Prison ~

Whereas, my attention has been called to the fact that shortly after her incarceration she gave birth to a child, said to be quite a bright boy, who, if left with his mother until the expiration of her sentence, would at this time be about 12 years of age, and would leave the prison without education and without intercourse with any one but convicts of the lowest order.

NOW THEREFORE, I, N.O. Murphy, Acting Governor of Arizona, in consideration of the facts as above stated, do by virtue of the power within me vested, and of these presents, grant unto the said M. Fimbrez, pardon and release from custody conditioned upon her immediately going beyond the boundary lines of this Territory, and that she forever remain outside its limits, otherwise this grant of freedom and pardon shall be void and of no effect.

IN TESTIMONY WHEREAS, I have hereunto set my hand and caused the Great Seal of the Territory to be affixed. DONE at Phoenix, the Capital, this twenty-fourth day of September A.D., 1891.

N.O. Murphy

By the Governor.
E.B. Kirkland
   Assistant Secretary of Territory.

OFFICE OF
SUPERINTENDENT TERRITORIAL PRISON
OF ARIZONA

Murray McInernay
  Superintendent

Yuma, Arizona, Sept. 25, 1891

I, M. McInernay, Superintendent of the Territorial Prison of the Territory of Arizona, do hereby certify that I received the annexed proclamation granting a Pardon to Manuela Fimbrez, conditioned that she immediately go beyond the limits of Arizona Territory, on the 24th day of September 1891, and that on the said 24th day of September aforesaid, I released her from this Prison, and placed her in charge of a competent person, Paul Moroney, Jr. Who agrees to see that she goes beyond the lines of said Arizona Territory.

I also certify that I delivered to her a copy of this proclamation and explained to her its intent and meaning, and the consequences to her if she ever returns to Arizona Territory.

M. McInernay
Supt. Territorial Prison

Manuela Fimbres

TERRITORIAL PRISON AT YUMA, A.T.

Description of Convict

NAME:
  Manuela Fimbres
ALIAS:

CRIME:
  Murder
COUNTY:
  Pima
LEGITIMATE OCCUPATION:
  Housekeeper

HABITS:
  Intemperate

OPIUM:
HEIGHT:
  4' 10"
SIZE OF HEAD:

COLOR EYES:
  Dark
MARRIED:
  Single

CAN READ:
  Yes (poorly)
WHERE EDUCATED:

NUMBER:
  572
SENTENCE:
  15 years
  3/30/1889
NATIVITY:
  Mexico
AGE:
  21
TOBACCO:
  Yes

RELIGION:
  Catholic

SIZE FOOT:
WEIGHT:
  101-1/2 lbs.
COLOR HAIR:
  Dark
CHILDREN:

CAN WRITE:
  Yes

FORMER IMPRISONMENT:

NEAREST RELATIVE:
  Mrs. Guadalupe Cira (Sic)

WHEN AND HOW DISCHARGED:
Conditional pardon by Gov. Murphy, 10/1/1891
Full pardon by Governor Murphy, March 30, 1904
Brought in by Sheriff Shaw

☙ Frail Prisoners in Yuma Territorial Prison ❧

PRISON RECORD

April 6, 1889 (From Arizona Sentinel)

Manuela Fimbres and Juan Enrique of Tucson were convicted of murder and were brought to the penitentiary by Sheriff Shaw on Saturday last. The prisoners killed a wealthy Chinaman last December after which Enrique fled to Sonora but was a short time afterwards captured. He is sentenced to 30 years imprisonment and the woman 15 years.

November 2, 1889

Manuela Fimbres, the Tucson woman, convicted of being an accessory to the murder of a Chinaman last Spring and sentenced to 15 years imprisonment in the Territorial Prison gave birth to a baby boy last Monday. She has been an inmate of the penitentiary since March 28. (date of birth of baby must be October 26.)

~ Jennie McCleary ~

Chapter 5

Jennie McCleary ~ No. 919

On June 18, 1893, Jennie assaulted Lulu Lee with a straight razor, which is considered to be a most deadly weapon, and certain to cause great bodily injury.

Lulu Lee filed a criminal complaint against Jennie, charging her of the crime of Assault with a Deadly Weapon; the act being committed on June 18, 1893. A warrant of arrest was issued on June 20, 1893, by D.R. Prime, justice of the Peace. Lulu Lee swore that Jennie McCleary, with intent then and there, feloniously, willfully, and of malice aforethought, to kill and murder her.

The Grand Jury of Coconino County examined the witnesses to the incident. They called Lulu Lee, W.W. Stout, R.M. Francis, Matt Blakely, Jennie McCleary, and W.S. DeClass to testify. Upon completion of their hearing they indicted Jennie on the charge of Assault with Intent to Commit Murder.

On October 24, 1893, Jennie pled not guilty to the indictment by the Grand Jury. When she was brought into court for trial she pled guilty to the charge of Aggravated Assault which

Frail Prisoners in Yuma Territorial Prison

was accepted by the court.

She was sentenced on November 3, 1893, by the court:

"You, Jennie McCleary, having been indicted by the Grand Jury of the County of Coconino, at the August Term, 1893, of this court of the crime of Assault with Intent to Commit Murder, to which indictment upon your arraignment, you plead guilty to the crime of Aggravated Assault on the 25th day of October A.D. 1893.

Have you anything to offer as legal cause why judgment and sentence should not be pronounced against you?

No legal cause being by you shown, or appears the judgment of the court is, that you, Jennie McCleary, are guilty of the crime of Aggravated Assault and the judgment and sentence thereon is, that you be punished therefore as follows to wit: That you, Jennie McCleary, be confined and imprisoned in the Territorial prison at Yuma in the Territory of Arizona for a period of one year and six months and that your term of imprisonment begin on the 3rd day of November, A.D. 1893.

Jno J. Hawkins, Judge

District Court of the Fourth Judicial District of the Territory of Arizona in and for the County of Coconino."

Jennie served her sentence with the exception of the last three months. She was recommended for pardon by the Superintendent and Assistant Superintendent of the prison because of exemplary conduct and the fact that she had acted as laundress in the prison since her confinement. Consideration was given to her youth and her promises that she will absolutely refrain from strong drink (and hopefully straight razors) and join her parents in Los Angeles immediately upon her release.

Governor Hughes gave her an unconditional pardon on November 29, 1894

Page 312 in court record: Oct. 26, 1893

On motion of the District Attorney the defendant was

~ Jennie McCleary ~

brought into Court for trial, being duly represented by counsel. Upon the statement of Counsel for the defense that the defendant desired to enter a plea of Aggravated Assault. The Court by permission of the Dist. Atty., admits the plea and hereby fixes the hour of 10 o'clock a.m. of Friday, November 3rd, A.D. 1893 for passing sentence.

The defendant was thereupon remanded to custody to await sentence.

Page 369 in court record: Nov. 3, 1893

Territory of Arizona vs. Jennie McCleary No. 57.

In this cause this day to wit: the 3rd day of November, A.D., 1893, having been fixed by the court for passing sentence on the defendant, Jennie McCleary, she was brought into court and her counsel W.G. Stewart, Esq. and H.Z. Zuck, District Attorney, being present and defendant standing in court, the following judgment and sentence was pronounced by the court and ordered entered:

You Jennie McCleary, having been indicted by the Grand Jury of the County of Coconino, at the August Term, 1893, of this court of the crime of Assault with intent to commit murder, to which indictment upon your arraignment, you plead guilty to the crime of Aggravated Assault on the 25 day of October A.D. 1893.

Have you no anything to offer as legal cause why judgment and sentence should not be pronounced against you.

No legal cause being by you show, or appears the judgment of the court is, that you, Jennie McCleary are guilty of the crime of Aggravated Assault, and the judgment and sentence thereon is, that you be punished therefore as follows to wit: That you Jennie McCleary be confined and imprisoned in the Territorial prison at Yuma in the Territory of Arizona for a period of One year and Six months and that your term of imprisonment begin on the 3rd day of November, A.D. 1893.

Jno. J. Hawkins, Judge
In the District Court of the Fourth Judicial District of the Territory of Arizona in and for the County of Coconino.

Frail Prisoners in Yuma Territorial Prison

RECEIPT FOR PRISONER

OFFICE of the SUPERINTENDENT of PRISON

Received of J.J. Donahue Sheriff of Coconino County Jennie McCleary sentenced for theCrime of Aggravated Assault for the term of One and one-half years by Hon. J.J. Hawkins of Court of said County.

DESCRIPTION: Height 5 ft, 5 in; Color Hair Black
Color Eyes Black; Marks on Body Scar on left shoulder.
No. 919

                                        Thomas Gates
                                        Superintendent of Prison

Jennie McCleary

TERRITORIAL PRISON AT YUMA, A.T.
Description of Convict

NAME:
   Jennie McCleary (Negro)
ALIAS:

CRIME:
   Aggravated Assault
COUNTY:
   Coconino
LEGITIMATE OCCUPATION:
Cook - Laborer
HABITS:
   Intemperate
OPIUM:
   No
HEIGHT:
   5' 5"
SIZE OF HEAD:
   6-1/2
COLOR EYES:
   Black
MARRIED:
   Widow
CAN READ:
   Yes
WHERE EDUCATED:
   Kansas (Public)

NUMBER:
   919
SENTENCE
   18 mos. from 11/3/1893
NATIVITY:
   Lexington, Kentucky
AGE:
   27
TOBACCO:
   Yes
RELIGION:
   Baptist
SIZE FOOT:
   6-1/2
WEIGHT:
   117 lbs.
COLOR HAIR:
   Black
CHILDREN:

CAN WRITE:
   Yes
FORMER IMPRISONMENT:

NEAREST RELATIVE:
   Cherdie Jones, Emporia, Kansas

WHEN AND HOW DISCHARGED:
Unconditional Pardon by Gov. Hughes, November 29, 1894.
Brought to prison by Sheriff J.J. Donohue.

PRISON RECORD

Expression - open
Forehead - low
Mental Culture - slight.

Peculiarities in build and features - tall and slim built; face, pox-marked; nose, prominent and lips thick and protruding.

Scars - Scars on left hand and wrist and on right shoulder.
    Carriage - erect   Condition of teeth - Fair

The Yuma Times - Nov. 15, 1893 - (in part) Mrs. Jennie McCleary will serve 18 months for aggravated assault. She is almost a full blooded negress and gives her age as 27 years. Material was furnished her and she soon had herself arrayed in a dress of the regulation prison stripe.

Pardon recommended by the Superintendent and Assistant Superintendent of the prison on account of exemplary conduct and in consideration of the fact that she has acted as laundress in the prison since her confinement. The applicant has served all but three months of her sentence and in consideration of her youth and promise and pledges that she will absolutely refrain from strong drink and join her parents in Los Angeles immediately upon her release.

November 28, 1894

Chapter 6

Georgie Clifford~No. 947

Peter Perry turned up dead in a house of ill repute in Williams, Arizona on December 26, 1893. His death was caused by morphine believed to have been administered by Georgie Clifford.

The Grand Jury of Coconino County indicted Georgie for murder on March 15, 1894. The indictment read:

"That the said Georgie Clifford, on the 26th day of December, A.D. 1893, at the County of Coconino and Territory of Arizona, did feloniously, unlawfully and with malice aforethought administer to and cause to be taken by Peter Perry into his body a deadly quantity of a certain deadly poison, called morphine, she, the said Georgie Clifford, then and there well knowing the same to be in quantity and kind as so administered and taken, a deadly poison; by means of the taking of which deadly poison into the body of the said Peter Perry he, the said Peter Perry became then and there mortally sick, and distempered in his body, of which mortal sickness and distemper of body the said Peter Perry then and there instantly died; and so the said Georgie Clifford did in manner and form aforethought kill and murder the said Peter Perry."

Georgie plead not guilty to the charge and her trial began on May 22, 1894.

Amy Powell, the keeper of the house of ill fame, testified that a woman, named Lillie Taylor, served all the drinks taken by Peter Perry. There was no proof that Georgie gave him even one drink on that fateful night.

The evidence presented also identified Lottie Williams as the person who made a hypodermic injection on Perry. The evidence showed that Lottie had been habitually addicted to the use of morphine for at least ten years. And she kept a supply of morphine all the time along with a hypodermic syringe for her own use. Lottie Williams fled the country and though the county sheriff made a search for her in California, he was unable to locate her.

Georgie testified that Lottie showed her where she had injected Perry. The defendant said she had left Lottie with the victim at a late hour. When she returned she found Lottie trying to revive Perry. When Perry died, Georgie awoke the denizens of the house and then went to summon Dr. Johnson.

No matter what was presented at the trial the jury found Georgie guilty of manslaughter. She was 20 years old. Lottie Williams was 38.

"Territory of Arizona vs. Georgie Clifford, No. 92

You, Georgie Clifford, having been indicted by the Grand Jury of the County of Coconino, at the March Term 1894, of this court of the Crime of Murder, to which indictment upon your arraignment you plead not guilty, and put yourself upon the country, and by that country, to-wit; by the verdict of twelve good and lawful men you were found guilty of the Crime of Manslaughter on the 22nd day, March, A.D. 1894.

Have you now anything to offer as legal cause why judgment and sentence should not be pronounced against you?

No legal cause being by you shown or appearing, the judgment of the Court that you Georgie Clifford are guilty of the crime of Manslaughter and the judgment and sentence therein that you be punished therefore as follows, to-wit:

Georgie Clifford

That you Georgie Clifford be confined and imprisoned in the Territorial Prison at Yuma, in the Territory of Arizona for a period of Three Years and Six Months and that your time of imprisonment shall begin on the 24th day of March, 1894.

Jno. J. Hawkins
Judge"

By the time Georgie had served eleven months of her sentence, Governor Hughes pardoned her unconditionally stating the following:

a. Her conduct in prison was exemplary.
b. She was the only female prisoner which made her confinement solitary.
c. It appeared that she was not the chief offender in the crime and that the more guilty party had escaped.

Her pardon was effective February 22, 1895. Georgie did not just disappear into the limbo of time and history as did most of Yuma's frail prisoners. According to the Arizona Republican August 23, 1896, she appeared before Justice Johnstone to file a complaint against Frank Serrano. She claimed that she had $100 in gold and had wanted to go out drinking. Serrano talked her into letting him keep her gold safe while she was partying. Georgie agreed--but when she returned to claim her $100 he denied that she had given him any money. In fact he insinuated that she was still drunk or dreaming. Johnstone told her that she had no proof that Serrano had her $100 in gold and refused to issue a warrant. This incident established her as Georgia Redmond for the first time.

The Arizona Republican,   May 5, 1897 wrote:

"Two women were arrested on Sunday afternoon for violent assaults on men, both committed at about the same time. Georgia Redmond, a morphine fiend, cut Henry Rubenstein, and Leo DuBois tried to break Victor Balleter's skull with a beer bottle."

A later paper said that she, Georgia Redmond, was lodged

in jail, a pitiable object. She claimed that she only used her knife after Rubenstein had knocked her down. The paper went on to say that she would likely be sent to the insane asylum. It also related that she had served time in Yuma for killing a man a few years back. At the time of her release from prison she was a very strong, physical woman. The police tried to arrest her one night--but she knocked four of them down and hit the fifth so hard that he was unconscious for some time.

The newspaper was right. On May 6, 1897, the probate court adjudged her insane and committed her to the asylum. They believed that she had really tried to kill Rubenstein, the tailor with whom she had been living.

During her court hearing she appeared in very sad condition; emaciated and untidy. Her peers believed that she was a dangerous woman--to society and to herself.

When the death of Perry was discussed she maintained that she didn't give him the poison. She said that another woman had killed him then fled. When the authorities were unable to find the real culprit they turned to her because they had to punish someone.

The court and the doctor had a problem as to what to do with her. They would not accept an addict at the hospital or the county jail. Georgia cried and begged them not to send her to the asylum. But they did.

Meanwhile, being cut up put Rubenstein into the public eye. On May 8, 1897, councilman Dennis filed a complaint against him for keeping a "disorderly house," at the corner of Washington and Second streets. Mr. Dennis lived across the street. Rubenstein came into court with a bundle of women's dresses and an old account book as proof as to why women came to his cleaning and dying business. John Dennis swore that all kinds of women, but good women visited at all times of day and night. The police court convicted Rubenstein of keeping a disorderly house.

When he appeared for sentencing, Rubenstein was asked if he had anything to say. And he had plenty. He disclosed that he had a wife and seven children living in Florida.

Evidently, his greatest ambition was to cure Georgia of the "dope habit." His remedy for cure was to give her all she wanted until she was sick of it. At first the cost was 40 cents a day; then it grew to 50 cents. Finally, Georgia's demands for cocaine cost him a dollar a day. Unsuccessful in this venture turned him to drink.

"I vas vonce," he said, "a happy man, a postmaster mit a hundred dollar a mont ven Drant vos de president. Now, I am vot you see. I shtood high up."

He had spent $1,100 in less than a year trying to cure Georgie Redmond. Now he had 80 cents in his pocket, some secondhand clothes, a wife and seven children, and a bad memory of when he stood high up. Unimpressed, the court fined him $20 but gave him time to raise the money.

Once in Rubenstein could not stay out of trouble. On August 23, 1897, he heard that shortly after being released from the asylum Georgia had taken another lover. He threatened the man with death, then went home to get a pistol. The police caught him with it before he found his victim. On August 24th the court fined him $90 for carrying a concealed weapon.

Then an astounding event took place. It was reported by the Arizona Republican, October 1, 1897:

"Henry Rubenstein and Stella Campbell were married yesterday afternoon at 5 o'clock at Mr. Rubenstein's residence on East Washington Street. The ceremony was performed by Justice Kincaid."

Author's note: Stella Campbell was also Georgia Clifford. Campbell may have been her real name. Henry Rubenstein served 90 days in jail because he could not pay the $90 fine.

If the marriage made Georgia happy it was not for long. Her sad end was reported in the Arizona Republic, October 24, 1897.

Georgia Redmond, a character known in every mining camp in Arizona, died last night at the Florence Criftenton rescue home. She died as a result of the use of morphine and cocaine; being almost a maniac from its use.

The dead woman is about 23 years old, coming to Prescott from Missouri about six years ago. At the time she had a husband and baby. She began to use narcotics and liquor; was sent to Yuma for poisoning a man. After her pardon she served two terms in the asylum.

Georgie Redmond

The Arizona Republican   May 5, 1897

Georgie Redmond, the morphine fiend, who cut Henry Rubenstein last Sunday, is in jail, a pitiable object. Her case is set for hearing before Justice Johnstone today. She says that she wielded the knife after Rubenstein had knocked her down. She will more likely be sent to the insane asylum than be returned to jail. She served a term at Yuma for killing a man at Prescott a few years ago. When she was released from prison she was a woman of powerful physique. She lived at Tucson and one night got into a conflict with the authorities. They tried to arrest her and do it without violence. After she had knocked four men down, a heavy member of the force sailed in. She put her fist on the point of his jaw and he lay on the ground so long that if he had been in a prize fight he would have been counted out.

May 4, : Two women were arrested on Sunday afternoon for violent assaults on men, both committed at about the same time. Georgia Redmond, a morphine fiend, cut Henry Rubenstein, and Leo DuBois tried to break Victor Balleter's skull with a beer bottle.

⁓ Georgie Clifford ⁓

May 6, 1897

SENT TO THE ASYLUM: A Proceeding Showing a Great Deal of Goodness In This World.

    Georgia Redmond, the young woman arrested last Sunday on a charge of trying to kill Henry Rubenstein, a tailor called "the professor: with whom she had been living at the corner of Washington and Third streets, was adjudged insane in probate court yesterday and was committed to the asylum. Her trial on the original charge was set for yesterday morning before Justice Johnstone. He continued the case until the afternoon and in the meantime made complaint against her in probate court. She is a victim of both the morphine and cocaine habits. She was sent to the asylum early last fall and was discharged as cured. She was sent to the penitentiary at Yuma nearly four years ago for murder. She served eighteen months and when she was released she was a model of health and strength. When she was brought into court yesterday she was as nearly a physical wreck as a living woman may be. She was emaciated, the skin drawn tightly over the bones of her face and her hair was merely a dirty yellow thatch.
    Dr. Duffield conducted the examination of the witnesses, Deputy Sheriff Boyd and Justice Johnstone. Both believed that she was a dangerous woman under the influence of the drug and that she took it in such quantities that her own life was in constant peril.
    In reply to questions by the doctor she said she began taking it about four years ago. After her release from the penitentiary she resumed the habit. Regarding her penitentiary experience Sheriff Orme said that she was sent there for poisoning a man. She had given him a dose of morphine out of the effect of which he passed into eternal rest.
    "I didn't give it to him," interrupted the prisoner, "another woman gave it to him and when they couldn't find her they took me because they wanted to punish somebody." She evened matters up with the sheriff by finding fault with the

menu of the jail which she said was no better than that of the asylum. She begged that she might not be sent there. She would rather be sent to the penitentiary or permitted to remain in jail. "At the asylum," she said, "all those crazy women are afraid of me but I wouldn't hurt them. I never hurt anything in my life, and never wanted to. But they'll put me in handcuffs again. "She ran away from there two or three times last fall," said the sheriff. "I didn't run away, " she retorted, "I just walked off and came to town."

She cried bitterly while the doctor and the probate judge were discussing her case. Something would have to be done with her. They had been criticized, they said, for sending this class of cases to the asylum. But what else could be done with them? They could not be sent to the hospital and they could not be kept in the county jail. The patient brightened up and came to the relief of the puzzled judge and doctor with a solution which seemed to be simple. "Let me go!" she cried. Justice Johnstone and the doctor talked to her. They told her they were only anxious that she might be finally cured. They promised to see the superintendent of the asylum and tell him to treat her kindly and let her go as soon as she was cured. If Mr. McKinley should get a wiggle on himself soon and appoint a governor who would appoint another superintendent, they would see him too, and have her good treatment continued.

She quit crying and said she was ready to go.

The scene was not a wholly pleasant one, but the tender interest which the witnesses and the officials manifested in her case, the steadfast purpose to rescue a woman who had fallen to the lowest depths, was convincing that the world is a great deal better and more tender hearted than many people think it is.

May 7, 1897:

Georgia Redmond, the morphine and cocaine fiend, adjudged insane on Wednesday afternoon, was taken to the asylum yesterday. She is persona non garat there, not because the superintendent is not sympathetic, but because he believes the asylum was not intended for that class of cases. The patients in the first place, he says, are not insane within the meaning of the word as it is commonly understood. They are much more troublesome than any other patients and are practically incurable with the facilities afforded at the asylum. If they could be kept there six months or a year they might be cured. But it is impossible to keep them beyond that period when they are restored to sound mind. Ninety-nine out of a hundred of them, the doctor says, go back to the habit again soon after their discharge. He says, moreover, that these patients are not sent from any other part of the territory than Phoenix.

May 8, 1897

When Henry Rubenstein escaped punishment in Justice Johnstone's court for contempt the other day, he was still not out of the woods. Yesterday morning Councilman Dennis made complaint against him for keeping a disorderly house at the corner of Washington and Second streets, just opposite Mr. Dennis' residence. All of the "Professor's" trouble grows out of his getting cut last Sunday and the consequent disclosure of just what sort of a place he was maintaining.

Georgia Clifford

The Arizona Republican   **May 11, 1897**

Henry Rubenstein was convicted in police court yesterday of keeping a disorderly house. Sentence was suspended two days. The case was set for 3 o'clock. The recorder did not come until ten minutes after and Maurice B. Fleishman, one of the attorneys for the defense, moved to dismiss on that ground. Mr. Rubenstein brought into court a bundle of women's dresses and an old account book as exhibits by which he intended to prove that women called at his cleaning and dying establishment on legitimate business. John T. Dennis swore that all

Frail Prisoners in Yuma Territorial Prison

kinds of women but good women visited Mr. Rubenstein's place night and day. Mr. Davis, in a mixture of broken German and Italian, said that on the day that Mr. Rubenstein got cut, just as he got to the door he met Dolph Liebenow coming out with a bloody knife. Mr. Liebenow is a respectable gentleman who happened to be passing and hearing the screams of the woman, Georgia Redmond, broke down the door and separated her and Rubenstein and took the knife from her. The crowd in the police court did not know this and Mr. Davis reference to him and the bloody knife seemed to implicate Mr. Liebenow. His friends roared with delight and he exhibited embarrassment. Mr. Davis tried to continue his narrative but clung tenaciously to Mr. Liebenow and the knife. "Well, well," said Mr. Liebenow, "jog along with your story and get through with it." Mr. Davis continued, "We a him and me get a de woman out on' a we gif a her our advice to pull a her freight, she pull a out."

May 13, 1897:

LIFE OF RUBENSTEIN: Pathetic Story of an Uncompleted Reformation.

Henry Rubenstein, the professor, was in police court yesterday afternoon to receive sentence for keeping a disorderly house, of which he had been convicted two days before. Mr. Rubenstein was asked if he had anything to say why sentence should not be passed upon him. Mr. Rubenstein had a great deal to say; so much that it looked for awhile as if the proceedings would have to be continued to another day. Mr. Rubenstein's remarks comprised a very complete biography of himself from his earliest recollection. His narrative began with the incidents of the cutting affair at his house on Sunday a couple of weeks ago. There had he said, at one time or another, been a great deal of noise about the place, but he himself had seldom spoken above a whisper. The high average of tumult of which the neighbors complained was attained by Georgia

Redmond, the cocaine fiend, who made much more noise than two persons might be expected to create.

Mr. Rubenstein said that notwithstanding he had a wife and seven children living in Florida, the highest ambition of his life came to be to break Georgia of the "dope" habit. To that end he had endeavored to make her sick of the stuff, give her her fill of it. He began expending 40 cents a day for cocaine, then 50 cents. Georgia's capacity for the drug grew with her opportunity and at last Mr. Rubenstein's outlay for cocaine alone was a dollar a day. Here he saw the futility of his patent method for breaking up the cocaine habit and he took to drinking hard himself.

Mr. Rubenstein spoke of his wife and children without much feeling, but when he talked of Georgia Redmond, he was deeply moved.

"You are done with her now forever," said the recorder.

"Foreffer," replied Mr. Rubenstein in a choked whisper. His disgust was apparently unutterable and he didn't try to utter it, but indicated it by a broad backward sweep of his hands. He sat down and wept, but a minute later arose dry eyed, and continued the story of his fall. "I was vonce," he said, "a happy man, I vos a postmaster mit a hundred dollar a mont ven Drant vos bresident. Your honor, I vos not vat you see now. I shtood high up." (Mr. Rubenstein is now only about five feet four.) In a vain attempt to describe his former social altitude he held his hands as far as possible above his head. That was not high enough and he stood on tip-toe. He was still something short of his former grandeur and he began climbing upon a chair, when the recorder stopped him and said he understood the awful height from which he had descended.

His attempt to reform Georgia Redmond had cost him in one way and another $1,100 within a year. Now he had nothing except 80 cents in cash, a lot of second-hand clothes, his wife and seven children and the bitter memory of former prosperity. He yet had hope and the habits of a money maker and would try to redeem the errors and correct the mistakes he had made since his residence in Arizona. The court fined him $20 and gave him plenty of time to raise the money.

✼ Frail Prisoners in Yuma Territorial Prison ✼

The Arizona Republican   **May 26, 1897**

Georgia Redmond, the cocaine fiend, ran away from the asylum yesterday. Dr. Hughes telephoned to town inquiring about her and at last located her in Tempe. He sent a carryall after her and she was brought back last night. The drug was taken away from her a week ago. Since then she has brightened greatly and is gaining in flesh rapidly. She was admitted to as much freedom as possible. Yesterday morning she was allowed to be on a porch with other inmates. Suddenly she disappeared barefoot and bare headed.

June 26:

Georgia Redmond, made insane by the use of opium and cocaine and sent to the asylum two months ago, was discharged yesterday.

August 24:

Henry Rubenstein is "strictly in it." That is, he is in trouble, in jail, and in default of the amount of a $90 fine imposed upon him in police court yesterday for carrying a concealed weapon. Then again a warrant has been issued against him from Justice Kincaid's court. It will be served when the city has fully wreaked its vengeance upon him. The beginning of all Mr. Rubenstein's woe was jealousy. Some one told him that another man had supplanted him in the affections of Georgia Redmond, who was the source of a great deal of sorrow to him early in the summer. Rubenstein found the offender and threatened him with death. He went back to his place of business after a gun with which to carry out his threat. He set out again breathing slaughter. In the meantime the intended victim was not standing still. He appealed to the authorities for protection and Jailor Duncan went prospecting from Rubenstein. When Rubenstein saw him he ran into a saloon and was in the act of handing the gun to the bartender when the officer arrested him. Rubenstein made the usual plea for mercy, the usual confession of his unworthiness and the usual promise to reform. The heart of the recorder was unapproachable as Mr. Rubenstein himself is now and will before the ensuing ninety days unless he pays the fine.

Oct. 1 1897: Henry Rosenstein and Stella Campbell were married yesterday afternoon at 5 o'clock at Mr. Rosenstein's residence on East Washington street. The ceremony was performed by Justice Kincaid.

Georgia Redmond

Arizona Republican   **Sept. 2, 1897**

H. Rosenstein is wearying of his ninety days' confinement in the city jail for carrying concealed weapons. Yesterday he addressed an appeal to Recorder Jobs setting forth the following facts, many of which are self evident or known to be true: In the first place he is in jail; in the next place he is a dyer and cleaner in possession of a place of business containing several hundred dollars' worth of second-hand clothing. Thirdly, his confinement interferes with the prosecution of his avocation to such an extent that his business house is temporarily closed. Fourthly, he is embarrassed and his affairs are in a critical situation. Fifthly, his rent is long over due and his landlord is likely to be afflicted with impatience, seeing his tenant is in jail. Mr. Rosenstein believes that now that the cool season is approaching, second-hand clothing will be in demand. If he had access to it, he thinks, he could sell enough of it to pay the rest of his fine on installments.

Georgie Clifford

Sentence: Territory of Arizona vs. Georgie Clifford No. 92

You, Georgie Clifford, having been indicted by the Grand Jury of the County of Coconino, at the March Term 1894, of

Frail Prisoners in Yuma Territorial Prison

this Court of the Crime of Murder, to which indictment upon your arraignment you plead not guilty, and put yourself upon the country, and by that country, to-wit: by the verdict of twelve good and lawful men you were found guilty of the Crime of Manslaughter on the 22nd day, March, A.D. 1894.

Have you now anything to offer as legal cause why judgment and sentence should not be pronounced against you?

No legal cause being by you shown or appearing, the judgment of the Court that you Georgie Clifford are guilty of the crime of Manslaughter and the judgment and sentence therein that you be punished therefore as follow, to-wit:

That you Georgie Clifford be confined and imprisoned in the Territorial Prison at Yuma, in the Territory of Arizona for a period of Three Years and Six Months and that your time of imprisonment shall begin on the 24th day of March 1894.

Jno. J. Hawkins
Judge

Receipt for Prisoners Office of the Superintendent of Prison Yuma, A.T. March 26, 1894

Received of J.J. Donahue, Sheriff of Coconino County Georgie Clifford sentenced for the Crime of Manslaughter for the term of Three and one-half years by Judge of District Court of the said County.

Description: Height 5 ft, 6 1/4 in; Color Hair Dark Brown Color eyes: Grey; Marks on Body small scar on left side of mouth.

No. 947   *Thomas Gates*
                                    Superintendent of Prison

PROCLAMATION OF PARDON

Territory of Arizona, Executive Department

TO ALL TO WHOM THESE PRESENTS SHALL COME GERRTING:

    Whereas, Application for pardon has been made to this Department by Georgia Clifford a convict in the Territorial Prison, who was tried and convicted of the crime of Manslaughter at the March term A.D., 1894 of the District Court of the Fourth Judicial District in and for the County of Coconino; and was sentenced therefor to imprisonment in the Territorial Prison for the term of 3 years, 6 months the sentence to date from March 24, 1894.

    Whereas the application for pardon is recommended by Supt. of Prison, and Board of Prison Commissioners on the grounds of exemplary conduct and for the further reason that the said Georgia Clifford is the only female prisoner at present in confinement in the Prison, maker her confinement virtually solitary.

    It further appearing that the applicant was not the chief offender in the crime for which she is imprisoned, and that the more guilty party had escaped.

    Now, Therefore, I, LOUIS C. HUGHES, by virtue of the power and authority in me vested do hereby grant unto the said Georgia Clifford a full and unconditional Pardon and do order that she be set a liberty 22 February.

    IN TESTIMONY WHEREOF, I have this 19th day of February set my hand and caused the Great Seal of the Territory to affixed. Done at Phoenix, the Capitol, this 19th day of February 1895.

By the Governor Louis C. Hughes
Charles M. Bruce
Secretary of the Territory.

⛧ Frail Prisoners in Yuma Territorial Prison ⛧

Georgie Clifford #947

Arizona Republican   October 24, 1897

GEORGIA REDMOND DEAD:
The End Came of Morphine at Crittenton Home.

Georgia Redmond, a character known throughout almost every town and mining camp in Arizona, died last night at the Florence Crittenton rescue home. Death was indirectly, if not directly the result of morphine and cocaine. Three days ago she was taken in a helpless condition from her lodging to the home. One Sunday afternoon last June, attention was first attracted to her by her cutting L. Rosenstein, with whom she had irregularly living. She was arrested and taken to the county jail. She was almost a maniac from the use of cocaine and morphine. The next day she was charged with insanity, tried in probate court and committed to the asylum. The remained a couple of months and was discharged, not as cured for no insane asylum here a year before and was similarly discharged. She returned to town in August and for a time tried to withstand temptation. At length she gave away.

The dead woman is about 25 years old. She came to Prescott from Missouri with a husband and baby six years ago. She was separated from her husband, who obtained control of the child. After that she began using narcotics and liquor. About a year later she was sent to Yuma from Yavapai county for murdering a man by poison. She was pardoned a couple of years later and that pardon was her ruin. Her descent after that was swift, interrupted only by the two terms in the asylum.

TERRITORIAL PRISON AT YUMA, A.T

Description of Convict

NAME:
   Georgie Clifford
ALIAS:
   Stella Campbell
CRIME:
   Manslaughter
COUNTY:
   Coconino
LEGITIMATE OCCUPATION:
   Laborer
HABITS:
   Intemperate
OPIUM:
   Yes
HEIGHT:
   5' 6-1/2"
SIZE OF HEAD:

COLOR EYES:
   Gray
MARRIED:
   Yes
CAN READ:
   Yes
WHERE EDUCATED:

NUMBER:
   947
SENTENCE:
   3-1/2 yrs. from 3/24/1894
NATIVITY:
   South Carolina
AGE:
   20
TOBACCO:
   No
RELIGION:
   Protestant
SIZE FOOT:
   6
WEIGHT:
   130 lbs.
COLOR HAIR:
   Dark Brown
CHILDREN:
   None
CAN WRITE

FORMER IMPRISONMENT:

NEAREST RELATIVE:
   Has parents, yes
   No relative listed

WHEN AND HOW DISCHARGED:
   Unconditional Pardon by Governor Hughes, February 22, 1895.

PRISON RECORD

Peculiarities in build - Slim built. Regular features. Scars - Small scar on left side of mouth. Syringe marks on both legs. Complexion - Light   Expression - Open   Forehead - High   Carriage - erect   Condition of teeth - good.
From Physician's Report - April 1, 1895
   The female patient No. 947, Georgie Clifford, who had been under treatment fot the morphine habit was pardoned during the quarter. At the time of her discharge though, a complete cure had not been effected. The daily allowance had been reduced from eight grains to less than a grain of the drug.

☙ Frail Prisoners in Yuma Territorial Prison ❧

Isabelle Washington

Chapter 7

Isabelle Washington~No. 1103

Little can be said of this woman except that she was callous enough to give birth to a baby then throw the helpless infant into an irrigation canal in Tempe.

The Grand Jury indicted her for murder on November 9, 1895. Isabelle plead not guilty to the murder charge.

However, on November 14, 1895, she withdrew her not guilty plea and re-entered a plea of guilty to the crime of manslaughter.

Washington was sentenced to one year in the Territorial Prison, her sentence beginning on November 15, 1895. She was 19 years old and could not read or write.

She served her sentence in Yuma and was released on September 14, 1896. Nothing more was heard about her.

Isabelle Washington #1103

Criminal Register of Actions   Maricopa County, Arizona
The Territory of Arizona
No. 659   vs
1895   Isabelle Washington

Murder

Date
Oct. 14   Filed compl, Warrant, List of Witnesses, Transcript, 2 exhibits, Docketing.

Nov. 7   Ent. appearance before Grand Jury
     9   Indicted for Murder
        Filed and entered Indictment

Nov. 11   Defendant arraigned
          Ent. appearance of deft. for arraignment
          Order setting time to plead.

Nov. 12   Demurrer to Indictment, Overruled, (Deft. to plead)
          Ent. appearance of Deft to plead.
          Filed demurrer to Indictment
          Ent. order o.r. demurrer.

Nov. 13   Pleads "Not Guilty"
          Ent. appearance of deft. to plead

Nov. 14   Withdraws plea of "not guilty" and pleads guilty to the crime of Manslaughter.
          Ent. order, Withdrawal of plea of "not guilty."
          Ent. order setting time for sentence.
          2 p.m. for sentence.
          Ent. order continuing to 9 a.m. tomorrow.
          Sentence continued to 9 a.m. Nov. 15

Nov. 15   Ent. appearance of Deft for sentence
          Defendant sentenced to one year in Territorial Prison from November 15th, 1895
          Ent. Judgment
          Issued commitment.

Isabelle Washington

TERRITORIAL PRISON AT YUMA, A.T.
Description of Convict

NAME:
  Isabelle Washington
ALIAS:

CRIME:
  Manslaughter
COUNTY:
  Maricopa 19
LEGITIMATE OCCUPATION:
  Seamstress
HABITS:
  Temperate
OPIUM:
  No
HEIGHT:
  5' 1-1/2"
SIZE OF HEAD:
COLOR EYES:

MARRIED:
  No
CAN READ:
  No
WHERE EDUCATED:

NUMBER:
  103
SENTENCE:
  1 yr. from Nov. 15, 1895
NATIVITY:
  Missouri
AGE:

TOBACCO:
  No
RELIGION:
  Methodist
SIZE FOOT:
  4-1/2
WEIGHT:

COLOR HAIR:
CHILDREN:
  Yes
CAN WRITE:
  No
FORMER IMPRISONMENT:

NEAREST RELATIVE:
  Has parents (Brothers)
  Henry Washington,
  Salem Co., Missouri

WHEN AND HOW DISCHARGED:
  By expiration of sentence, September 14, 1896

PRISON RECORD

Slender built   Scrofla (sic) scar on left side of neck.
Carriage - erect   Condition of teeth - fair.
November 23, 1895   Arizona Sentinel

Sheriff Orme of Phoenix arrived here last Saturday with Isabelle Washington (colored) sentenced to the Territorial Prison for one year under plea of builty of Manslaughter for having thrown her newly born babe in the canal at Tempe.

⚘ Frail Prisoners in Yuma Territorial Prison ⚘

Susie Smith

Chapter 8

Susie Smith~No. 1125

CRIMINAL REGISTER OF ACTIONS
MARICOPA COUNTY, ARIZONA

	The Territory of Arizona
NO. 676	vs.
	Susie Smith

1895 Date	Receiving Stolen Property
Nov. 20	Indictment for Receiving stolen property Filed and entered indictment Order for Bench Warrant, Issued warrant
Nov. 21	Ent. appearance of Deft. for arraignment - Deft. Arraigned Ent. order setting time to plead Ent. order fixing bail. To plead Nov. 22nd 9 a.m. Bond fixed at $1000.00 to be approved by clerk
Nov. 22	Subp. for Amy Wildman (sic) & 3 wit. endt. Nov. 23rd Subp. for J.B. McNeil & 2 wit. endt. Nov. 23rd. Ent. appearance of deft. to plead. Pleads "Not Guilty." Ent. order setting case for trial. For trial Nov. 23rd, 9 a.m.
Nov. 23	Issued subp. for Wm. Tyner & 8 Pres. req. Nov. 25 (sic)

55

Nov. 25	Ent. appearance of deft. for trial. Ent. order for Jury and trial of case. Screening and impanelling Jury Screening 4 witnesses for pros. Case tried, verdict, "Guilty as Charged." 3 witnesses for Deft. Filed 3 exhibits Swearing bailiff for Jury Lackland Receiving and recording verdict Filed verdict, Jury list, Instructions Ent. order remanding for sentence
Nov. 26	Appearance of deft. for sentence Ent. order continuing order (sic) fixing bail.
Nov. 27	Ent. appearance of deft. Filed and entered motion for new trial Ent. order setting hearing of motion 3 p.m. Ent. appearance of deft 3 p.m. Ent. order denying motion for new trial Ent. Judgment. Deft. Sentenced to one year in Territorial Prison Ent. order extending time to make up statement of facts. Defendant granted 30 days to make up statement of facts. Issued commitment
Dec. 3	Ent. order for return of exhibits to Dr. Scriggs (sic)

~ Susie Smith ~

TERRITORIAL PRISON AT YUMA, A.T.

Description of Convict

NAME:
: Susie Smith

ALIAS:

CRIME:
: Receiving stolen property

COUNTY:
: Maricopa

LEGITIMATE OCCUPATION:
: Cook

HABITS:
: Temperate

OPIUM:
: No

HEIGHT:
: 5' 5-1/2"

SIZE OF HEAD:

COLOR EYES:
: Black

MARRIED:
: Single

CAN READ:
: Yes

WHERE EDUCATED:
: Louisville (Private School)

NUMBER:
: 1125

SENTENCE:
: 1 yr. from Nov. 27, 1895

NATIVITY:
: Kentucky

AGE:
: 27

TOBACCO:
: No

RELIGION:
: None

SIZE FOOT:
: 7

WEIGHT:
: 152 lbs.

COLOR HAIR
: Black

CHILDREN:

CAN WRITE:
: Yes

FORMER IMPRISONMENT:

NEAREST RELATIVE:
: Mother - Martha Ash, Dallas, Texas

WHEN AND HOW DISCHARGED:
: Pardoned by Gov. B.F. Franklin, Sept. 20, 1896
Brought in by Sheriff Owens

PRISON RECORD

Scar - Small scar on top of head   Forehead - Medium
Carriage - erect   Condition of teeth - false.

RE: Pardon - and whereas the said application is made solely for the purpose of restoring the said Susie Smith to citizenship, and is endorsed by the Superintendent for the Territorial Prison, Sept. 19, 1896.

Arizona Sentinel - Sept. 26, 1896 - Governor Franklin last Saturday issued a pardon, releasing Susie Smith, the colored girl who was sentenced because certain stolen articles were found in her trunk. Her time, less credits for good behavior, would have expired today.

Arizona Republican - Sept. 20, 1896 - The Governor yesterday issued a pardon to Susie Smith, the colored girl, who was sentenced to serve one year in the penitentiary for complicity in the robbing of the Wildman residence at Tempe. Her time would have expired on the 26th inst.

◈ Teresa Garcia ◈

Chapter 9

Teresa Garcia ~ No. 1225

Robert Fraser made a complaint on August 3, 1896 that Roberto Gudino and Teresa Garcia did unlawfully enter the dwelling of William Tierney and did steal and carry away the good, chattels, and personal property in the dwelling.

Garcia took into her possession one gray dress shirt, valued at five dollars; one wrapper value of 75 cents; underclothing valued at ten dollars; one jewelry case, containing one watch and chain, one lot of gold finger rings, one lot of earrings, one gold puzzle ring, one lot of gold and ornaments and one lot of sleeve cuff buttons, aggregating in value, one hundred dollars; and one work box valued at five dollars; the total amounting to the sum of $125.75 in lawful money of the United States; all of which belonged to Alice Tierney.

William Scott, Justice of the Peace, released Roberto Gudino saying that there was not sufficient evidence to hold him. The Justice ordered Garcia held.

Following that the Grand Jury charged the defendant with the crime of receiving stolen goods for her own gain.

On September 26, 1896, Teresa entered a plea of not guilty. On October 6, 1896, a jury of her peers found her guilty as charged in the indictment. On October 7th she was sentenced to two years her term to begin on the same date.

Garcia was pardoned on October 7, 1896, because the prison did not have proper facilities for confining females and it was felt that she had been sufficiently punished.

Teresa A. Garcia

IN THE JUSTICE COURT

Precinct No. 1 County of Pima Territory of Arizona.
Robert Gudino and Teresa A. Garcia, Complaint-Criminal,
Before Wm. F. Scott, Justice of Peace.

Personally appeared before me, this 3rd day of August, 1896, Robert Fraser of the County of Pima, who, first being duly sworn complains and says: that one Roberto Gudino and Teresa A. Garcia did on or about the 5th day of July A.D., 1896, at and within the County of Pima, Territory of Arizona, commit the crime of Burglary, committed as follows to wit: The said Roberto Gudino and Teresa A. Garcia, did at the time and place aforesaid willfully, unlawfully and feloniously enter the dwelling house of Wm. J. Tierney then and there situated, with the intent then and there, unlawfully and feloniously & take, steal and carry away the personal property goods and chattels then and there in the dwelling house aforesaid. All of which is contrary to the form of the statute in such case made and provided, and against the peace of the people of the Territory of Arizona. Said complainant therefore prays that a warrant may be

Teresa Garcia

issued for the arrest of the said Roberto Gudino and Teresa A. Garcia and that they may be dealt with according to the law.

Robert Fraser

Subscribed and sworn to before me Wm. F. Scott this 3 day of August A.D. 1896. Justice of Peace

August 3, 1896

Amended complaint upon oath having been filed by Robert Fraser that the crime of burglary has been committed and accusing Roberto Gudino and Teresa A. Garcia thereof. Defendants being in Court, complaint read to defendants, who was duly informed of their rights and being ready for hearing. The following named witnesses was sworn and examined on part of the prosecution, Mrs. Allie Tierney. Mrs. Adelia Russell, F.W. Purcell and R. Fraser, defendants being duly informed in their rights, Roberto Gudino made a statement in his behalf, Teresa A. Garcia had no statement to make. It appearing to me that there is not sufficient evidence to hold Gudino. It is therefore ordered and adjudged that the defendant Teresa A. Garcia be held for having stolen goods in her possession knowing that the said goods was stolen, I order that she be held to answer the same, and that she be admitted to bail in the sum of $1000.00 and be committed to the custody of the Sheriff of the County of Pima until she give such bail.

Wm. F. Scott
Justice of Peace

Frail Prisoners in Yuma Territorial Prison

Territory of Arizona
    vs.   INDICTMENT
Teresa A. Garcia

    In the District Court of the First Judicial District of the Territory of Arizona in and for the County Pima. The eighteenth day of September 1896 Teresa A. Garcia is accused by the Grand Jury of the said County of Pima, by this Indictment of the crime of receiving stolen property for her own gain, knowing the same to have been stolen personal property, committed as follows:

    The said Teresa A. Garcia did on or about the fifth day of July, A.D. 1896, at, and within the County of Pima, Territory of Arizona, willfully, knowingly, unlawfully and feloniously, and for her own gain, receive and take into her possession the following described personal articles, to wit: One gray dress shirt of the value of five dollars, one wrapper of the value of seventy-five cents, underclothing of the value of five dollars, one set of silver knives of the value of ten dollars, one jewelry case containing one watch and chain, one lot of gold finger rings, one lot of ear-rings, one gold puzzle ring, one lot of gold and ornaments and one lot of sleeve cuff buttons, aggregating in value, one hundred dollars, and one work box of the value of five dollars, all amounting in value to the sum of one hundred and twenty-five dollars and seventy-five cents in lawful money of the United States of America all of which said personal property was then and there the property of and belonged to one Mrs. Alice Tierney, and all of which had been, therefore, and on or about or about said fifth day of July 1896, unlawfully, feloniously taken, stolen and carried away from her, the said Alice Tierney in said county and territory. And she, the said Teresa A. Garcia, then and there at the time she so received and took said personal property into her possession, as and for the purpose aforesaid well knew that the same and all thereof had been so stolen as aforesaid, then and there willfully, knowingly and feloniously and for her own gain received and took into her possession all of the personal property aforesaid.

Contrary to the form, force and effect of the Statute in such cases made and provided, and against the peace and dignity of the territory of Arizona.

                                          Wm. M. Lovell
                          District Attorney Pima County
                                                  Arizona

~ Teresa Garcia ~

Names of witnesses examinted before the Grand Jury upon the finding of the foregoing indictment:
Mrs. Alice Tierney, Robert Frazer, R.E. Paul

Minute entry of September 17th, 1896:

It is by the Court ordered that S.E. Buzzard be and he is hereby appointed to act as counsel for Teresa A. Garcia during the impanelment of the Grand Jury.

Now comes the Grand Jury and report a true bill of indictment charging the defendant herein with the crime of receiving stolen property for her own gain, knowing the case to have been stolen personal property, whereupon it is by the Court ordered that the clerk do furnish to the said defendant upon her arraignment in this action a copy of the indictment herein.

Minute entry of September 25th, 1896:

Now comes Teresa A. Garcia in person and by counsel R.D. Ferguson Esq. and the District Attorney being present thereupon the defendant was duly arraigned according to law, she stated through Richard Brady, a Spanish interpreter first duly sworn that her true name was correctly set forth in the indictment herein a true copy of which was handed her and thereupon defendant was allowed until tomorrow to plead.

Minute entry of September 26th, 1896:

Defendant brought into Court in custody, S.D. Ferguson Esq., counsel for defendant, and defendant plead "Not Guilty" as charged in the indictment; therefore the Court ordered that said cause be set for trial Tuesday, October 6th, 1896.

Minute entry of October 6th, 1896

Now comes the District attorney and the defendant in person and by her counsel R.D. Ferguson into Court, and announces ready for trial. Thereupon 24 jurors were called into the jury box and duly sworn according to law and from whom were selected twelve good and lawful men to wit: L.W. Crane, F.C. Morton, V.M. Cordova, C.F. Gooding, F.F. Winters, Naobr Pacheco, C.A. Elliot, S.B. Conley, D.J. Burrows, C.F. Brown, N.J. Spicer and W.C. Knox, who were duly sworn according to law then duly impanelled and sworn to try the issue joined between the Territory of Arizona and the defendant.

The following witnesses wee sworn, examined and cross-examined on the part of the prosecution to wit: Mrs. Alice Tierney, Mariana Laloux. The defendant was then sworn in her own behalf and the evidence closed.

Arguments were had by the counsels on both sides and the case submitted.

And now the jury having heard the evidence and the argument of counsels and the instructions of the Court given in writing and filed with the papers in the case, the jury retired in charge of the bailiff R. Pacheco (duly sworn for that purpose) to consider of their verdict. Subsequently the jury returned into Court and upon being asked if they had agreed upon a verdict reported through their foreman S.B. Conley as follows, "We the jury impanelled and sworn in the above entitled cause upon our oaths do find the defendant "Guilty as charged in the indictment." Whereupon the Court ordered said verdict recorded and the defendant remanded to the custody of the sheriff to appear before this Court for sentence on tomorrow morning Oct. 7th, 1896.

~ Teresa Garcia ~

TERRITORIAL PRISON AT YUMA, A.T.

Description of Convict

NAME:
    Teresa A. Garcia
ALIAS:

CRIME:
    Receiving stolen property
COUNTY:
    Pima
LEGITIMATE OCCUPATION:
    Laundress
HABITS:
    Intemperate
OPIUM:
    No
HEIGHT:
    5' 7-3/4"
SIZE OF HEAD:
    Black
COLOR EYES:
    Black
MARRIED:
    Yes
CAN READ:
    No
WHERE EDUCATED:

NUMBER:
    1225
SENTENCE:
    2 yrs. from
    Oct. 7, 1896
NATIVITY:
    Mexico
AGE:
    18
TOBACCO:
    Yes
RELIGION:
    Catholic
SIZE FOOT:
    2
WEIGHT:
    133-1/2 lbs.
COLOR HAIR:

CHILDREN:

CAN WRITE:
    No
FORMER IMPRISONMENT:

NEAREST RELATIVE:
    Has parents - yes
    Antonio Garcia,
    Rio Yaqui, Mexico

WHEN AND HOW DISCHARGED:
Pardoned by Gov. McCord, Oct. 7, 1897

PRISON RECORD

Forehead - Medium
Expression - open Carriage - erect
Condition of teeth - Good

Complexion - sallow
Build - short & stout

Written on Pardon: Teresa A. Garcia recommended for pardon by John Dorrington. That she has been sufficiently punished, and further the prison not having proper facilities for the confinement of females, they become subversive of prison discipline.

Frail Prisoners in Yuma Territorial Prison

Maria Moreno

Chapter 10

Maria Moreno ~ No. 1224

Arizona Sentinel   **July 4, 1896**

"MURDER: A Sister Kills Her Brother With A Shot Gun

The people living in the neighborhood of the corner of Maiden Lane and Fifth street were startled Tuesday morning about 10 o'clock by hearing the report of a gun and immediately afterwards heart rendering cries were heard. Some of the neighbors saw a young girl rush from one of the stick houses in that vicinity with a double barrel shot gun in her hand and on leaving the house brought it to her shoulder, there was a flash, a report and when the smoke cleared away, a young boy could be seen laying full length on the ground, with one side of his face blown off. The "she devil's" work accomplished, she threw the gun down beside the dead boy and turned to make her escape. The mother made her appearance on the scene and grasped her daughter by the hair and endeavored to hold her, but the frenzied murderess soon disengaged herself and ran through the saloon into an adjoining room where she remained until taken to jail by the officers.

The girl who had committed murder was Maria Moreno, aged 16 years, and the boy who laid on the ground in the burning and blistering sun, a victim of an ungovernable temper, was her brother, Alberto, aged 15 years.

It seems the boy had been reprimanding his sister for participating in the pascol dance, which was going on nightly next door, as she was doing things unbecoming a decent girl. She took offense at this and retaliated by calling him unmention-

Frail Prisoners in Yuma Territorial Prison

able names and in return he slapped her with a shoe. She instantly whirled and walked into the room where the shot gun was, and the boy started toward Gila street. Only a few yards had been traversed by him when his sister came out with the gun and called after him; "I am going to kill you." The brother turned about and in reply said, "Kill me." These were his last words on earth for hardly had they left his lips when she pulled the trigger with the above terrible results.

The boy bore the reputation of being a good and quiet lad and it is the opinion of all that the girl is to blame.

Considerable sympathy is expressed for the girl by those who know her and have employed her. It is their opinion that at times she is out of her mind.

The mother is a widow with several small children. She is nearly crazed with grief over the unfortunate affair.

The family has been suffering for the necessaries of life of late and only a few days ago Father Gheldof waited on a number of ladies and solicited funds with which to purchase food for them. He also called on the Board of Supervisors and we understand they promised to give $8 per month toward their support.

At the preliminary hearing Thursday before Justice Duke, the murderess was held over to await the action of the grand jury for murder without bail.

Gila Martinez and Martin Zavalla, principal witnesses, were put under bonds of $500 each. Failing to give the same they also languish in jail."

Maria plead not guilty to the terrible crime and was remanded to the custody of the sheriff on October 7, 1896.

Her trial was conducted and ended as expected with the unanimous decision by the jury--guilty of manslaughter.

Moreno was sentenced to the Territorial Penitentiary for the period of one year and one month on October 9, 1896. The jury had recommended her to the mercy of the court. Evidence presented revealed that she was weak minded as were all her younger brothers and sisters.

She served her sentence and was released.

~ Maria Moreno ~

Court Record of Maria Moreno

Wednesday, October 7th A.D., 1896

Now come the Grand Jury into Court and their names being called, all respond and report

  The Territory of Arizona)
     vs   ) Indictment for Murder
  Maria Moreno   )

  The Territory of Arizona)
     vs.   ) Indictment for Robbery
  George Wilson   )

and thereupon retire to further deliberate

  The Territory of Arizona)
     vs.   ) Indictment for Murder
  Maria Moreno   )

  Now comes the defendant in custody of the Sheriff into Court, and W.O. Huson (sic) her attorney, and the District Attorney being present, is arraigned.
  Defendant is asked her true name and replies, Maria Moreno. Whereupon the Indictment against her is read. A copy furnished her Counsel and the customary time to plead being waived, enters the plea of "not guilty" and the defendant is remanded to the custody of the Sheriff.
It appearing necessary that a Venire for trial jury should issue. It is ordered that the Sheriff summons ten good and lawful citizens of the County (and not bystanders) to be and appear in Court this day at 1 o'clock a.m. therein to serve as Trial Jurors.

The Trial Jurors heretofore summoned and in attendance are excused until 1 o'clock p.m., and all witnesses, likewise are instructed to return at that hour.

1 o'clock p.m.

≫ Frail Prisoners in Yuma Territorial Prison ≪

Comes the Sheriff and makes due return of persons summoned to serve as trial jurors.

    The Territory of Arizona   )
                vs.   )   Indictment Murder
    Maria Moreno   )

The defendant and respective counsel present.
The Jury is called, all respond and are sworn in statutory form to try the cause. The Indictment is read, plea thereto, stated, and Martin Zabala and Ygnacio Moreno sworn and examined on part of the prosecution and prosecution rests. Thereupon Ygnacio Moreno, L. Esselburn, S. Sumner (sic), U.G. Wilder, W.U. Elliot, B.A. Harazthy, H. Leonard, M.L. Pool and C. Cronin are sworn and examined as part of defense and defense rests. Ygnacio Moreno called by the prosecution in rebuttal. Counsel waives argument - instructions are given by the Court, and the Jury retire in the charge of an officer sworn for that purpose to deliberate upon the verdict.

    The Territory of Arizona   )
                vs.   )
    Maria Moreno   )

Now comes the Jury into the Court, their names called, and all respond. The defendant and respective counsel present. The Jury are asked by the Court if they have agreed upon their verdict, and reply, "aye" and hand to the Court the (?) which it ordered recorded to wit: For the District Court of the Third Judicial District of Arizona, County of Yuma. Note: Part missing

~ Maria Moreno ~

Thursday, October 9, 1896

The Territory of Arizona	)	
vs.	)	Murder
Maria Moreno	)	Manslaughter

Now comes the defendant in this case and is arranged for sentence. The Court informs said defendant of all the proceedings had in this matter against her from the findings of the Indictment against her by the Grand Jury to an including the present stage of proceedings and asks the defendant if she has any legal cause to show why the sentence of the Court should not now be passed upon her, and no legal cause being shown it is ordered, adjudged and decreed by the Court that the said defendant Maria Moreno is guilty of Manslaughter, and said defendant is therefore sentenced to be imprisoned in the Territorial Penitentiary of the Territory of Arizona for the period of one year and one month, and that the said term of imprisonment shall commence from this date, Dated October 9, 1896.

Court Record - Maria Moreno

List of Jurors:

Comes the defendant into Court and by her Counsel Brown & Huson the District Attorney present, and the proceeding to impanel the Jury to try the cause follows every requirement of the law and statue, and the persons remaining, to wit:

B.C. Heyl	C. Boyd
L. Leroy	O.B. Bloomer
H. Cantrell	F. Bassett
E.L. Crane	C. OBrien
T.D. Fordon	George Cachenberry
G.W. McMorris	W. Millar

are impanelled.

❦ Frail Prisoners in Yuma Territorial Prison ❦

The Jury are placed in charge of an officer for the noon repast, and (Part missing)

Arizona Sentinel   **October 10, 1896**

Court Proceedings: (In part)
    Maria Moreno - charged with murder. The jury brought in a verdict of manslaughter. About four months ago she shot and instantly killed her sixteen year old brother for no provocation whatever. She had been dissipating for some little time and keeping bad company. Her brother was expostulating with her when she took offense and killed him as above stated. The jury recommended her to the mercy of the court. The evidence went to prove that she was weak minded as are also her younger brothers and sisters. She received a sentence of one year and one month.

PRISON RECORD

Carriage - erect   Condition of teeth - Good
Stout built   Complexion - sallow
Expression - Downcast

Arizona Sentinel   **July 28, 1899**

Maria Moreno, a girl about twenty years of age, died Monday and buried Tuesday evening. Maria will be remembered as the girl who killed her brother some two or three years ago, for which crime she was sent to Territorial Prison for a year, which term she served. Maria was demented and was not responsible for her acts. She was talking to a man whose attentions her brother objected to and told her so. The girl became incensed at the reprimand and getting a shot gun fired at the brother, the charge tearing off the whole side of his face.

~ Maria Moreno ~

TERRITORIAL PRISON AT YUMA, A.T.

Description of Convict

NAME:
  Maria Moreno
ALIAS:

CRIME:NATIVITY:
Manslaughter
COUNTY:
  Yuma
LEGITIMATE OCCUPATION:

HABITS:
  Intemperate
OPIUM:
  No
HEIGHT:
  5' 5-1/2"
SIZE OF HEAD:

COLOR EYES:
  Black
MARRIED:
  No
CAN READ:
Yes
WHERE EDUCATED:
  Private A.T.
WHEN AND HOW DISCHARGED:
  Expiration of sentence

NUMBER:
  1224
SENTENCE:
  1 yr., 1 mo. from
  Oct. 9, 1896

  Arizona
AGE:
  16
TOBACCO:
  Yes
RELIGION:
  Catholic
SIZE FOOT:
  6
WEIGHT:
  155
COLOR HAIR:
  Black
CHILDREN:

CAN WRITE:
  Yes
FORMER IMPRISONMENT:

NEAREST RELATIVE:
  Has parents - Mother

⚘ Frail Prisoners in Yuma Territorial Prison ⚘

Trinidad Montano

Chapter 11

Trinidad Montano~No. 1254

On March 3, 1896, Officer Galpin arrested Joaquin Celaya for the theft of a trunk that belonged to Trinidad Montano. Following up on the woman's complaint, the officer found the disputed trunk in Celaya's possession. Officer Galpin made him take the trunk back to where he had gotten it. Celaya's excuse was that Montano owed him $2.25 and he had confiscated the trunk himself to save court costs.

Joaquin was put on trial in Justice Kincaid court. Montano had issued a complaint that he had taken her trunk and it was found in his room. In the courtroom her story changed. Now she swore she was drunk when she made the complaint and remembers that she had given Celaya the key to her room to take the trunk. Her new statement now cost her $14.70.

Marie Gilmore had been sentenced to a term in the county jail and while she was absent her home was robbed. On November 14, 1896, Constable Bayley happened to be in Tempe and saw one of the dresses answering the description of one stolen from the Gilmore home--on a Mexican woman, named Trinidad Montano. Obtaining a warrant, Bayley arrested Montano and Joaquin Celaya, too, as an accomplice.

Both were indicted for burglary. Both plead not guilty. Both demanded separate trials. Even with separate trials both were found guilty of second degree burglary. Both were sentenced to one year and nine months in the Territorial Prison on December 4, 1896.

John Dorrington recommended Montano's pardon on the

Frail Prisoners in Yuma Territorial Prison

grounds that she had been adequately punished and that the prison did not have the proper facilities for confining females. Governor Myron McCord complied and pardoned Trinidad Montano on October 7, 1897.

The Arizona Republican   **March 4, 1896**

Joaquin Celaya was put on trial in Justice Kincaid's court yesterday for burglary. A woman named Trinidad Montana had complained against him that he had broken into her room and carried off a trunk which was afterward found in his room when he was arrested. The woman went into court and swore that when she made the complaint she was drunk. When she sobered up she remembered that she had given Celaya the key to her room with authority to take the trunk away. Her new recollection of the affair cost her $14.70, the amount of cost which he had caused to accrue.

March 3, 1896 - Joaquin Celaya was arrested by Officer Galpin yesterday for stealing a trunk belonging to ?Trinidad Montano. The officer found the trunk in Celaya's possession. He made him take it back where it belonged and took him to jail. Celaya said the woman owed him $2.25. He issued himself an attachment and levied on the property to save court costs.

The Arizona Republican   **November 15, 1896**

DUAL MISFORTUNE   While in Prison, Marie Gilmore Has Had Her Wardrobe Molested.

Marie is serving a term in the county jail and during her enforced absence from her home her house was entered and several articles of wearing apparel stolen. This occurred several days ago. Yesterday Constable Bayley was in Tempe and

⚜ Trinidad Montano ⚜

on the person of a Mexican woman named Trinidad Montoya (sic) the officer saw a dress which strongly answered the description of one of the stolen dresses. He drove back to this city and secured additional evidence. Armed with a warrant the officer posted back to Tempe and arrested Miss Montoya and another woman named Joaquin Celaya as an accomplice. They were brought to this city and lodged in the county jail. Note: Joaquin Celaya is a man. Both were sentenced to prison for burglary.

COURT DOCKET No. 744

The Territory of Arizona vs. Joaquin Celaya and Trinidad Montano

Date   1896

Nov.   18   Filed and entered Indictment - Indictment for Burglary
             2 copies of Indictment 3 fol each
        19   Ent appearance of defts Joaquin Celaya and Trinidad Montano for arraignment.
             Ent order appointing counsel for Defts
             Ent order setting time to plead
             Ent appearance of each Deft to plead-Defts arraigned & each plead not guilty & demand separate trials.
             Ent order granting separate trials
             Ent order setting trial - Trial of Defts set for Nov 20th am
             Issued subp. For S.W. Bayley & 4
        23   Ent appearance of each deft for trial
             Ent order for Jury for trial of Trinidad Montano
             Swearing and impanelling jury
             Swearing Interpreter Manuel Garcia
             Swearing 5 witnesses for pros - Deft. Trinidad Montano trial
             Swearing 1 witnesses for deft   Verdict Guilty of burglary
             Bailiff for jury R.H. Drone (?)   in 2nd degree.
             Receiving & recording verdict
             Filed verdict   Jury list
             Ent order remanding Deft Montano for sentence
             Ent order setting trial of Deft Celaya - Trial of Deft Celaya

77

~ Frail Prisoners in Yuma Territorial Prison ~

		for Dec. 2nd.	set for Dec 2nd am
	24	Ent appearance of Deft Trinidad - Time of sentence of Montano	
		Montano	fixed for Nov. 25th
		Ent order setting time for sentence	
	25	Ent appearance of Deft Montano for sentence.	
		Ent order postponing sentence - Nov. 25th Sentence postponed	
	30	Issued for S.W. Bayley & 4	
Dec.	3	Ent appearance of Deft Celaya for trial	
		Ent order for Jury for trial of case	
		Swearing & impanelling Jury	Deft Celaya tried, Verdict guilty of Burglary in (?) degree
		Swearing Interpreter Manuel Garcia	
		Swearing 5 witnesses for pros	
		Swearing 4 witnesses for deft	
		Swearing Bailiff R.H. Drone (?)	Each deft ordered to appear for sentence Dec.4th
		Receiving & recording verdict	
		Filed Verdict Jury list	
		Ent order remanding deft & order for sentence	
		Ent order setting sentence for deft Montano - Dec. 4th, 1896.	
		Ent appearance of deft Joaquin Celaya	Each defendant sentenced to imprisonment in Territorial Prison for a term of one year and 9 months.
		Ent Judgment of deft Joaquin Celaya	
		Issued commitment of deft Joaquin Celaya	
	4	Ent appearance of Trinidad Montano for sentence	
		Ent Judgment of Trinidad Montano	
		Issued commitment	

PRISON RECORD

Forehead - Low   **Carriage - Erect**   **Teeth - Good**

Written on her pardon: Trinidad Montano recommended for pardon by John Dorrington. That she has been sufficiently punished, and further the prison not having proper facilities for the confinement of females, they become subversive of prison discipline.

She was tried on the same charge with Joaquin Celaya; he received the same sentence. #1257

~ Trinidad Montano ~

TERRITORIAL PRISON AT YUMA, A.T.

Description of Convict

NAME:
  Trinidad Montano
ALIAS:

CRIME:
  Burglary 2nd. Degree
COUNTY:
  Maricopa
LEGITIMATE OCCUPATION:
  Laborer
HABITS:
  Temperate
OPIUM:

HEIGHT:
  5' 1-3/4"
SIZE OF HEAD:
  6
COLOR EYES:
  Black
MARRIED:
  Yes
CAN READ:
  Yes
WHERE EDUCATED:
  Phoenix (Private)

NUMBER:
  1254
SENTENCE:
  1 yr. 9 mos. from
  Dec. 4, 1896
NATIVITY:
  Mexico
AGE:
  18
TOBACCO:
  Yes
RELIGION:
  Catholic
SIZE FOOT:
  4
WEIGHT:
  110 lbs.
COLOR HAIR:
  Black
CHILDREN:

CAN WRITE:
  No
FORMER IMPRISONMENT:

NEAREST RELATIVE:
  Francisco Montano
  Has parents: Both

WHEN AND HOW DISCHARGED:
  Pardoned by Gov. Myron H. McCord, Oct. 7, 1897

Frail Prisoners in Yuma Territorial Prison

Exie Sedgmore

Chapter 12

Exie Sedgmore~No. 1326

Lillian Harmon appeared before William Scott, Justice of the Peace, on September 7, 1897, and made a criminal complaint against Exie Sedgmore. She charged that Sedgmore assaulted her with a loaded revolver with the intent to do bodily harm.

The Grand Jury indicted Exie on September 14, 1897, for the crime of assault with a deadly weapon with intent to commit murder.

A trial was conducted and the jury reached this verdict: "We, the Jury impanelled and sworn in the above entitled cause, upon our oaths do find the defendant guilty of an assault with a deadly weapon upon the person of Lillian Harmon."

Frank L. Proctor, Foreman"

On October 1, 1897, Exie Sedgmore was sentenced to three years in the Territorial Prison.

By November 6, 1897, the Arizona Republican carried this notice:

"A petition is being circulated in Tucson to Governor McCord asking the pardon of Exie Sedgmore, who was convicted in the district court some time ago with assault to commit murder and sentenced to three years in the penitentiary. The petition has been signed by nearly all the business men. Miss Sedgmore, though that is by no means her name, was born and raised in Phoenix. Her maiden name was Ruiz and she married a respectable man here and lived with him several years."

Because of public feeling, Governor Myron McCord pardoned Exie on December 18, 1897, after she had served only 2 1/2 months of her three years sentence.

Frail Prisoners in Yuma Territorial Prison

In the Justice Court

Precinct No. One, County of Pima, Territory of Arizona

Territory of Arizona
    vs.   Complaint-Criminal
Exie Sedgmore

Before Wm. F. Scott   J.P.

Personally appeared before me, this 7 day of September, 1897, Lillian Harmon of Tucson, in the County of Pima who, first being duly sworn, complains and says: That one Exie Sedgmore on the 6 day of September A.A., 1897, at Tucson in the county of Pima, Territory of Arizona, did commit the crime of felony as follows to wit: the said Exie Sedgmore at the time and place aforesaid did unlawfully, willfully and feloniously assault said affiant with a deadly weapon, to wit, a revolver loaded with powder and ball with the intent to do bodily harm to affiant, all of which is contrary to the form of the statute in such cases made and provided, and against the peace of the people of the Territory of Arizona.

Said complainant therefore prays that warrant may be issued for the arrest of said Exie Sedgmore and that she may be dealt with according to law.

Subscribed and sworn before me, this 7th day of September A.D., 1897

                         Lillian Harmon
                         Wm. F. Scott
                         Justice of Peace

In the Justice Court, Precinct NO. One, Pima County, Arizona Territory, Transcript of Docket in the Cause of The Territory of Arizona vs. Exie Sedgmore - Felony.
September 7, 1897

Complaint upon oath having been filed by Lillian Harmon that the crime of Assault with a deadly weapon with the intent to do bodily harm to affiant has been committed and accusing Exie Sedgmore thereof.

A warrant for the arrest of Exie Sedgmore was issued and placed in the hands of R. Fraser, Constable for service.

~ Exie Sedgmore ~

INDICTMENT

Territory of Arizona
vs.
Exie Sedgmore

In the District Court of the First Judicial District of the Territory of Arizona in and fore the County Pima.

The 14th day of September 1897 Exie Sedgmore is accused by the Grand Jury of the said County of Pima, by this Indictment of the crime of assault with a deadly weapon with intent to commit murder committed as follows:

The said Exie Sedgmore did on the sixth day of September, A.D., 1897 at, and within the County of Pima, Territory of Arizona unlawfully, willfully, feloniously and with malice aforethought, make an assault in and upon the person of one Lillian Harmon with a deadly weapon, to wit: with a pistol then and there loaded and charged with gun powder and leaden balls, and then and there had and held in the hands of her the said Exie Sedgmore, and she the said Exie Sedgmore did then and there willfully, deliberately, unlawfully and feloniously shoot off and discharge the pistol so had, held and charged as aforesaid at and towards the person of her the said Lillian Harmon with the intent then and there willfully, deliberately, unlawfully, feloniously and with malice aforethought her the said Lillian Harmon to kill and murder, with the deadly weapon aforesaid, in the manner and form aforesaid.

Contrary to the form, force and effect of the Statute in such cases made and provided, and against the peace and dignity of the Territory of Arizona.

Thos. D. Satterwhite
District Attorney Pima County Arizona

Names of witnesses examined before the Grand Jury upon the finding of the foregoing indictment:
William Housten and Lillian Harmon.

Territory of Arizona
vs.
Exie Sedgmore

Now comes Frank H. Herefore, Attorney for the defendant herein, and makes affidavit that he as such attorney is acquainted with the facts connected with the defense of the defendant in this action. That Thomas Wilson, a resident of the City of Tucson, County of Pima, Territory of Arizona is a material witness for the defendant in this action. That the said Thomas F. Wilson is now in the state of California, and that from the best information that affiant can obtain, will not return to the County of Pima in Territory of Arizona until some time about the latter part of this month of September or the first part of the month of October of this year. That affiant has been informed and believes by the said Wilson and believes the said Wilson will testify that on the night of the shooting alleged to have taken place in the indictment herein, he, the said Thomas F. Wilson was lying in bed in his room directly across the street from the place where the shooting occurred and was there lying in bed awake when the shots were fired. That he heard nothing to indicate that any bullet had struck his said house in which he was as aforesaid lying at the time, and that next morning he examined the said house for bullet marks and was unable to find any thereon. That there were certain marks on the said building that might have been caused by bullets but that each and all thereof had been there for a long time previous to the night on which the shooting occurred. That affiant has been unable to find anyone by whom the above and foregoing matters of evidence can be proved, and that affiant believes that the testimony can be obtained from no other source that the said Thomas F. Wilson. The said Wilson as aforesaid is a resident of the City of Tucson, Pima County, Territory of Arizona. That the continuance sought to be obtained upon this affidavit is not sought for delay only, but that justice may be done.

Frank H. Hereford
Attorney for the defendant.

~ Exie Sedgmore ~

Register of Actions and Fee Book,
First District Court, Pima County
Arizona Territory

No. Suit A-935
Felony
Year 1897

Terry. Of Ariz. Plaintiff
vs.
Exie Sedgmore - Defendant
T.D. Satterwhite, Dist. Atty., Plaintiff's Att.
F.H. Hereford, Defendant's Att.

	Proceeding Had by Plaintiff		
Sept.		23	Ent ord trial
8	Docketing		Ent ord cont to 2 p.m.
14	Ent. Indictment		Ent ord Arguments
	Fil. Indictment		Swear Bailiff
	Ent. ord for copy		Order for meals
	Prepare copy		Ent & Fil verdict
15	Ent ord arraign.		Ent ord exec. Jury
	Ent plea "Not guilty"		Ent ord set sentence 27th
	Ent one set case for trial	28	Ent ord Cont. (?)
16	Ent ord to withdraw plea		Ent ord Cont. 2 p.m.30
	Fil Demurrer		
	Ent ord set 17th to plead		**Proceeding Had by Plaintiff**
17	Ent ord set 3 p.m. for	29	Ent ord cont case to Oct 1
	Demurrer		Fil. 6 papers N. Trial
	Ent ord Continuance (sic)	30	Ent ord (?) motion to Oct.
18	Ent ord overrule Demurrer		
	Ent ord 21st 2 p.m. to plead	Oct	
21	Iss. Subj. Annie Sullivan No. 2.D.	1	Ent ord overrule motion N.T.
			Ent ord overrule to
	Iss. Subp. W.V. McCleary D.		arrest (?) Judgment.
	Ent. plea N.G.		Ent ord to appear for Sent.
	Ent ord Set 22 for trial		Ent ord Judgment
22	Fil. 2 Subp.		
30	Fil Subp.		Iss Commitment
22	Ent ord trial		Fil same
	Swear & Imp. Jury		
	Ent ord cont (sic)		
	Swear witnesses 8		
	Order for Jury to return		
	Ent. order excuse Jury to 10 a.m.		

85

Subscribed and sworn to before me
this 20 day of September, 1897.

C.D. Hoover, Clerk
by AA Bernard (sic)
    Dpy.

Territory of Arizona, Plaintiff
vs.
Exie Sedgmore, Defendant
No. A-935

   We, the Jury impanelled and sworn in the above entitled cause, upon our oaths do find the defendant guilty of an assault with a deadly weapon upon the person of Lillian Harmon.

Frank L. Proctor, Foreman

Exie Sedgmore

Tucson, Arizona, November 9, 1897

TO THE GOVERNOR

Your Petitioner Represent:

There is now confined in the Territorial Prison at Yuma, one Exie Sedgmore who was convicted at the last term of the District Court for Assault with Intent to Kill and sentenced to the Prison for a term of three years. We, the Jurors who tried the case, and found her guilty, respectfully ask that you pardon her for the following reasons, viz.:

It is well known that the Yuma Prison has not accommodations of a character to properly keep a woman there. Further, Exie Sedgmore, while confined here after her sentence and previous to being sent to Yuma, suffered as keenly from the prospect before her, that we believe she has received a lesson which will effectually prevent any repetition of any such offense on her part. We know from reliable authority that the woman was in a hysterical and terrible state of mind during all the time, some five or six days after the judgment was rendered against her and before she was sent to Yuma, and we believe the ends of justice will be better subserved by pardoning her now when the full force and knowledge of the punishment meted out to people who commit the offense for which she is convicted, is still fresh in her mind, then if she is allowed to harden in the undesirable (for a woman) conditions of the Yuma Prison.

For these reasons as well as other, which we do not feel it necessary to dwell upon at this time, we most earnestly request that you pardon the said Exie Sedgmore and release her from further confinement in the Territorial Penitentiary.

F.L. Proctor	Foreman
J.J. Chishohn	Juror
N.E. Hawke	Juror
J.H. Burns	Juror
R.B. Kelley	Juror
J.M. Mariscal	Juror
James Flynn	Juror
M. King	Juror
C. Birkenfeld	Juror
Bob (sic) Baily	Juror
Vicente Lavoirie (sic)	Juror
Thos. D. Satterwhite	Dist. Atty.

Exie Sedgmore

TO THE GOVERNOR:

YOUR PETITIONERS REPRESENT:

That two women, Exie Sedgmore and Lillian Harmon, had quarreled and were at enmity; that the latter drove to the house of the former and their quarrel was renewed; that during this altercation, and after many bitter words had passed between them, the former, while standing in the front door of her own house, fired a revolver twice.

For this she was indicted, the indictment charging her with an assault on Miss Harmon and deliberately shooting at her.

At the trial of the case it was claimed by the prosecution that Miss Sedgmore deliberately shot at Miss Harmon, and with the intent to kill her; whereas the defense insisted that the shots were purposely fired in the air and were only fired to frighten. The fact that the opposite side of the street is bounded by a high and a solid adobe wall; that the street is a very narrow one; that the hack stood immediately in front of the door in which Miss Sedgmore stood at the time she fired the shots, and that Miss Harmon was then in the hack; and that, after the most careful and diligent search no trace of either bullet could be found, seems to corroborate the theory and claim of the defense. Nevertheless, the jury, after long deliberation, returned a verdict of "guilty of an assault with a deadly weapon upon the person of Lillian Harmon;" and the Court thereafter sentenced Miss Sedgmore to three years in the penitentiary at Yuma.

In signing this our petition we do not wish to be construed as favoring the settlement of private differences with the aid of fire arms; but in view of all the facts and circumstances of this case; of the further fact, of which we are well assured, that the real object in the punishment of crime is to prevent crime, and to maintain and assert the majesty of the law, then both objects have been fully subserved by this conviction and sentence, for it has already broken the spirit of this poor woman, and has carried to the minds and consciences of evil disposed persons the solemn warning to them; and in view of the further fact, upon which we beg to be understood as placing our chief emphasis, that at the Penitentiary at Yuma it is impossible to hold a woman either in a fit, a proper or moral way; and, therefore, the life of a woman in that institution, is as great, if not greater, crime than the one charged against this poor woman.

It is for these reasons that we unite in earnestly urging you to pardon EXIE SEDGMORE.

RESPECTFULLY

V.H. Matas M.D. (sic) Atty.
Charles F. Neiyer (sic)
Joe Manciet   Constable
Thomas F. Wilson
H.H. Pease
A. Orifla
F.M. Smith
M.B. Purcell M.D.
S.W. Purcell, atty.
J.S. Wood   Probate Judge
John E. Mayer - mining man

E.E. Ellingwood, U.S. Dist
C.W. Wright
William F. Cooper
S.E. Hazzard
Thos. A. Boston
Jos. J. Perry
N.W. Fermer
Wm. H. Scott
W.H. Culver
Chas. Conard
Frank D. Treah

Chas G. Hoff
Thos. L. Bullock
A.B. Sampson Mill and Mine owner - Ex County Recorder
F.F. Winter   Member Grand Jury
W.H. Taylor   Under sheriff
R.W. Leatherwood   Sheriff
C.A. Ghibell   Recorder
Sam W. Finley   City Marshal
A.A. Lysight   Mining Clerk
Robert Fraser   Constable
Julian M. Franklin   atty-at-law
W.G. Power   Ex Court Reporter
F.A. Odermatt   Dentist
Jno. M. Compton   Deputy U.S. Marshal
F.K. Miller   Attorney
Geo. W. Oaks

Frail Prisoners in Yuma Territorial Prison

Another petition containing the same script was signed by the following:

F.E. Murphy	Florentz L. Winter (sic) . . .	member
W.A. McNeil	W.W. Miller	member
Joe Goldten (sic) . . . . .member	J.H. Martin	Grand juror
S.H. Drachman . . . . . .member	Fred W. Cooper.	Grand juror
C. Christensen . . . . . . .member	Geo. F. Meek.	Grand juror
Bernabe C. Brishta . . . .member	T.F. Avery Foreman	Grand juror
W.S. Neff . . . . .member	Douglass Snyder	Grand juror
Isidor Meyer . . . . .member	Geo. F. Kitt, member of . .	Grand Jury
Henry Meyer . . . . . . .member	J.P. Hohusen (sic)member of	Grand Jury

Another petition of the same script was signed by 205 citizens.

Office of Treasure of Pima County

Tucson, Arizona, Dec. 17th, 1897

Hon. Myron H. McCord
 Governor of Arizona
  Phoenix, Arizona

My Dear Sir:

In the matter of a pardon for Miss Exie Sedgmore I wish to say that in my opinion Miss Sedgmore did not deserve the severe punishment inflicted upon her. I have known her for a number of years and she has always been an exceptionally quiet and well-behaved woman. This was her first trouble in Tucson to my knowledge and it was a great surprise to me to hear of her difficulty. However, whether innocent or guilty, she has suffered a severe penalty already and I assure you that if you will pardon her at an early day, that the community will approve of your action.

Trusting that you will favorably consider the matter, I remain for Justice.

Very Truly Yours
Chas. G. Hoff.

Exie Sedgmore

Exie Sedgmore

Tucson, Arizona, December 17, 1897

Hon. Myron H. McCord,
Governor of Arizona
Phoenix, Arizona,

My dear Governor:
    This letter will be handed you by Miss Eva Blanchard who comes to you upon a mission of mercy. She will make an appeal to you for the pardon of her friend Miss Exie Sedgmore, who was sentenced sometime ago by the Court here to an imprisonment of three years in the Territorial Prison at Yuma. The facts in the case will undoubtedly be placed before you for your consideration, consequently it is unnecessary for me to say anything on that score. If the offense of which Exie Sedgmore was guilty, demanded punishment, at all, there is no doubt but she has amply paid the penalty, and should be released from incarceration in such a place as Yuma penitentiary is. There is a widespread feeling of sympathy for her here, and her pardon will undoubtedly meet with general approval by all who know of the circumstances.
    Miss Blanchard has worked unceasingly ever since the conviction of her friend, to secure her liberty. Her loyalty and devotion should be rewarded, and if, without infringement upon your ideas of right and justice, you can grant the request which Miss Blanchard will make of you, I for one, shall feel that you have done as act of worthy charity.

Very Sincerely Yours,
William F. Cooper.

PROCLAMATION OF PARDON

Territory of Arizona
Executive Department

To all to Whom these Presents Shall Come, Greeting:

WHEREAS, Application for Pardon has been made to this Department by Exie Sedgmore a convict in the Territorial Prison, who was tried and convicted of the crime of Assault with Intent to Kill at the Sept. Term, A.D. 1897, of the District Court of the First Judicial District in and for the County of Pima; and was sentenced therefor to imprisonment in the Territorial Prison for the term of Three years, the sentence to date from Oct. 1st, 1897.

WHEREAS, The application for pardon was recommended by The District Attorney who prosecuted the case; by eleven of the twelve jurors the case; by sixteen of the Grand Jurors who presented the indictment; by a majority of the business men of the city of Tucson where she resided and by a large number of the legal and medical profession of the city of Tucson and by most of the county officers of Pima County and most of the city officers of the city of Tucson and by a very large number of citizens.

Now, Therefore, I, Myron H. McCord, Governor of the Territory of Arizona by virtue of the power and authority in me vested, do hereby grand unto the said Exie Sedgmore a full and unconditional Pardon, and do order that she be set at liberty forthwith.

In Testimony Whereof, I have this 18th day
of Dec., set my hand and caused the Great
Seal of the Territory to be affixed.
Done at Phoenix, the Capital, this 18th day of Dec., 1897.

By the Governor Myron H. McCord

Charles H. Akers
Secretary of the Territory

~ Exie Sedgmore ~

TERRITORIAL PRISON AT YUMA, A.T.

Description of Convict

NAME:
   Exie Sedgemore
ALIAS:

CRIME:
   Assault w/deadly weapon with intent to commit murder
COUNTY:
   Pima
LEGITIMATE OCCUPATION:
   None
HABITS:
   Intemperate
OPIUM:

HEIGHT:
   5' 2-1/2"
SIZE OF HEAD:
   Black
COLOR EYES:
   Black
MARRIED:
   Yes
CAN READ:
Yes
WHERE EDUCATED:
   Arizona (Private)

NUMBER:
   1326
SENTENCE:
   3 yrs. from Oct. 1, 1897
NATIVITY:
   California

AGE:
   25
TOBACCO:
   No
RELIGION:
   None
SIZE FOOT:
   4
WEIGHT:
   135 lbs.
COLOR HAIR:

CHILDREN:
   1
CAN WRITE

FORMER IMPRISONMENT:

NEAREST RELATIVE:
   Mrs. Eva Blanchard (friend)

WHEN AND HOW DISCHARGED:
   Pardoned unconditionally by Gov. McCord, Dec. 18, 1897

PRISON RECORD

Condition of teeth - Good
Complexion - Olive Forehead - High
Build - Short, medium stout

Frail Prisoners at Yuma Territorial Prison

Women prisoners in Yuma had no special quarters, cells, or section until November, 1897. Until then quartering, feeding, and protecting these denizens of the prison was extremely difficult without the proper accommodations.

Resolution passed by the Board of Control:

"Resolved that the superintendent of the prison be, and is hereby instructed to construct two or more cells in the residence of the Assistant Superintendent or elsewhere for the safekeeping and accommodation of female prisoners and to employ a lady to act as matron, said matron to be paid a salary of not more than $50 per month."

The Arizona Sentinel, August 28, 1897, wrote:

"Assistant Superintendent Aspinwall of the prison is the only ladies' man on the hill. It is his duty to look after the wants of the female convicts of whom there are three, of more or less dangerous characters who have heretofore been a source of much annoyance and displeasure to the guards and management, owing to their scrapping proclivities. In some manner, however, the assistant superintendent, either by his kindness, good looks, or winning ways, has won the confidence and good graces of the frail prisoners, and now they will not even speak to anyone else connected with the management of the institution. Mr. Aspinwall has promised to have their wearing wardrobe replenished as their wearing apparel is somewhat frayed, and even behind bars they have not lost any of that feminine pride, a desire to dress as well as anybody. The assistant superintendent proposes to see that the girls are dressed as well as possible under the circumstances, but says they will have to leave off the frills of fashion until they are released from his care."

Arizona Sentinel, October 23, 1897:

"Superintendent Dorrington has begun the work of constructing new quarters for the female convicts in the Territorial Prison. The guards house occupying the northwest corner of the prison site is being remodeled and will be furnished with steel cells. When completed the new quarters will be in the charge of a matron, and the female prisoners will then be accorded all the conveniences usually found in such institutions and they will have no further cause for complaint.

Arizona Sentinel, November 13, 1897:

"The steel cells being placed in the new female quarters on the N.W. corner of the prison grounds will be completed next Monday and the frail prisoners installed therein. The new quarters are admirably located, remote from the other prisoners, overlooking the Colorado River and the city. The building is a two story structure with cells above and a neat work room on the ground floor where the prisoners will be employed during the day at work that suits their fancy. Under these conditions, with the careful attention of a matron the weaker prisoners will have ample opportunity to reform, if there is any reform left in them."

Excerpt from the Report to the Governor September 1, 1899:

"The women's department is about 30 by 30 feet in the southwest corner."

Frail Prisoners in Yuma Territorial Prison

" . . .When she was young and knew no sin, Before the tempter entered in . . ."

" . . .the money I had would have taken me back to liberty, decency, and happiness. . ."

96

Chapter 13

Pearl Hart~No. 1559

McClintock wrote in his "Arizona, the Youngest State,"... "In 1899 Arizona rejoiced in the possession of a female bandit, Pearl Hart, who carried shooting irons and who robbed stages. She was a woman of the half-world, with an insatiable craving for morphine, cigarettes and notoriety."

Pearl was described as a delicate, dark haired woman with refined features, a rosebud mouth, clear blue eyes, weighing slightly over 100 pounds, with a slight, graceful body.

On July 15, 1899, the Globe stage reached Cane Spring about the middle of the afternoon. Henry Bacon, the driver, stopped the horses for a brief rest. Two road agents stepped from concealment shouting, "This is a hold up! Keep your hands high in the air!"

While the larger bandit held the driver and passengers under his gun, the smaller gathered up the valuables, taking the driver's pistol, money, and jewelry and the passengers likewise. Securing their loot, the bandits rode south.

Bacon unhooked one of the stage horses and returned to Globe to report the holdup to Sheriff W.T. Armstrong. Posses went into action at once. The bandits headed for Benson, intending to catch the train out of the area. Unfortunately for them, they stopped to rest in a thicket of brush. Officers from Benson were notified and discovered the two asleep in the thicket. They found a man and woman who gave the names Joe Boot and Pearl Hart.

They were taken to Florence for a preliminary hearing and held without bail until they could go before the grand jury. The local jail had no facilities for women, so Pearl was sent to the Pima County Jail in Tucson. While awaiting trial on an indictment in the United States court for robbing the Globe-Phoenix stage last spring, Pearl Hart, the female bandit broke jail at 3:00 a.m. October 12, 1899.

The jail break is best described by the Tucson Star, October 20, 1899:

"Early yesterday morning Pearl Hart, the woman stage robber, escaped the county jail, and at this writing has not been captured. Pearl Hart was a prisoner of the Pinal County officials, but was taken from the Florence jail and brought to this city, as the accommodations at the Pinal County jail are not suitable to women prisoners. Since her confinement here Sheriff Wakefield and his deputies have used every precaution for her safekeeping, and they naturally feel much chagrined over her escape. Since her confinement in the Pima County jail, Pearl Hart has occupied a room directly over the rear room of the county recorder's office. This room adjoins the small room containing the stairway leading up to the tower of the building. A door opens from the small room on the second floor of the courthouse, at the head of the stairs leading down to the main entrance. Between the two rooms mentioned there is nothing but a lath and plaster partition. The door leading into the tower from the courthouse is generally locked, but on the night of the escape it apparently was not. It is evident that after everything was quiet someone entered the courthouse, walked up the stairway and entered the tower room through the unlocked door. It was the work of but a very few minutes to cut a hole through the wall into Pearl Hart's room. She held a sheet to catch the plaster that fell on her side. After the hole was cut through she put a table underneath, and placing a chair upon that, crawled through the hole. From the size of the aperture it is evident that Pearl Hart must have required considerable help in getting through. After joining her accomplice in the escape it was only necessary to open the door and descend the stairway into the street. As there is no night watchman for the courthouse outside the jail, it was an easy matter to gain the street without detection. In all probability, horses were in waiting and the pair made a beeline for the border. It is claimed that she may have left the city on the westbound passenger train but this is hardly a possibility as the risk of detection was too great. To those who have seen Pearl Hart either in her proper attire or the masculine dress she commonly wore, it can readily be imagined how difficult disguise would be. Ed Hogan, serving a sentence for drunk and disorderly conduct, is also missing and the theory is that he assisted Pearl in her escape. He had but ten more days to serve and had been given some liberty as a trusty. When the jail was locked up on Wednesday night Hogan was missing and it is presumed that he hid himself in the city until about midnight and then returned to the county building to assist in the escape, an understanding having been reached during his confinement as the method of escape.

Pearl Hart has added another chapter to her remarkable experience of the past few months, but whether she will be successful in remaining out of jail for any length of time remains to be seen. It was reported on the street late last night that Pearl has been captured afoot and alone on the road between here and Florence. None of the jail officials, however, knew anything of the reported capture."

Pearl was actually arrested by George Scarsborough in Deming, New Mexico, along with Ed Hogan, who helped her

Frail Prisoners in Yuma Territorial Prison

escape the Tucson jail. They had been slowly working their way east and had spent a few days in Lordsburg--but had not been recognized or else the officers of the law were not too anxious to recapture them.

Scarsborough recognized Arizona's female bandit from a photograph of her that he had seen in the Cosmopolitan magazine. She was arrested dressed in men's clothes and was transported back to Tucson in that manner. The entire town of Deming turned out to see her off on the train.

In November, 1899, Hart was tried for the stage hold up. The trial was held in Florence, and although she had admitted her guilt in writing, the jury acquitted her by a vote of 11 to 1. Judge Fletcher Doan was livid at the manner in which Pearl flirted with the jury, bending them to her will. Doan discharged that jury, had her re-arrested for stealing the driver's pistol and with a new jury found her guilty. She was sentenced to five years in the Territorial Prison beginning her term on November 17, 1899.

Joe Boot had a separate trial, but was also found guilty of holding up the stage and sentenced to 30 years. The officers' opinion of Boot was not very high as they described him thusly: "Boot is a weak, morphine, depraved specimen of male mortality, without spirit and lacking intelligence and activity. It is plain that the woman was the leader of this partnership."

Hart did not deny that statement and had nothing for Joe Boot but contempt. "Why the fellow hadn't an ounce of sand. While I was going thru the passengers his hand were shaking like leaves. He was supposed to be holding the guns. Why if I hadn't more nerve than that I'd jump off the earth!"

She did not seem dismayed over the prospect of a prison sentence in Yuma. "I shall make no defense," she said, "I don't care what the world does with me. I would do it all over again if I had the chance."

Hart was carrying all their money when she and Boot were captured. "In just one more day I would have reached the train going east. In another day I would have been home, my life here left behind forever. The money I had would have taken me back to liberty, decency, and happiness."

On sentencing Joe Boot went to the Territorial Prison to serve his 30 years--but he did not tarry there long. He was a model prisoner and soon became a trusty. Patiently, he waited his opportunity and when it came on February 6, 1901, he escaped and disappeared into Mexico forever. Boot had served less than two years.

During most of her sentence Pearl was the only woman at the prison and she made the most of it. Isolated as she was, she knew she had no opportunity to escape, but she did know that women were frequently paroled or sometimes pardoned. With thought toward freedom, she enlisted the help of her mother and sister, to assist her in the petition for parole to Governor Alexander O. Brodie. In this petition they made much of the fact that should Pearl be released she would be given the leading role in a play called "The Arizona Bandit." This play had been written by her sister and was to be presented on the Orpheum circuit depicting Harts' adventures as a stage robber.

While she was in prison Pearl was cured of the opium habit, for in the beginning she was a "hop fiend" of insatiable appetite. She always blamed Joe Boot for their capture and would have avoided it had he listened to her.

Pearl grew lonesome in prison and wanted the little pups just born to the dog, Judie. They would be company for her, but Ira Smith, the owner refused saying, "Judie is a lady and her pups are well bred and I don't want their morals contaminated by Pearl."

Hart wrote poetry in prison--a lot of poetry. One title was, "The Girl Bandit." Another was about her innocent (?) childhood that went:

When she was young and knew no sin
Before the tempter entered in

Pearl Hart's parole was recommended by the Board of Control and the Prison Superintendent. If the truth were known the governor was most anxious to be rid of Pear, but only if she would go away from Arizona Territory and stay away. Hart accepted these conditions and she was released from the Territorial Prison on December 2, 1902. She had served approximately 3 years of her 5 year sentence.

As an actress she never had much of a career, but her name became well known in the early 1900s when the silver screen released a movie called "Yuma City" regaling her experiences as a female bandit.

Late in 1903 she was known to be running a cigar and tobacco stand in Kansas.

Arizona Sentinel   December 17, 1902

"PEARL HART FREE:

THE NOTORIOUS WOMAN BANDIT WILL TACKLE THE STAGE AGAIN, THIS TIME AS AN 'ACTRESS' AND NOT AS A HIGH-WAY ROBBER"

Pearl Hart, the notorious, once more breathes free air, having been paroled by Governor Brodie last Saturday, and she left on Monday night's train for Kansas City. Quite a large number of people were at the depot to get a glimpse of Arizona's famous female ex-convict, and they were not disappointed for she was there, and if there is one thing more than another that Pearl is "shy on" it is a fondness for notoriety.

Her ticket was bought straight through to Kansas City, where her mother and sister live, and the latter has written a drama in which Pearl will assume the leading role, arrangements having been made to play the Orpheum circuit, the initial performance to be given in Kansas City. It is understood that the drama will embody Pearl's own experience as a stage robber, with all the blood and thunder accompaniments and the famous Pearl will, once again with her trusty Winchester, hold up the driver of a western stage, line up the passengers and relieve them of their valuables while her partner "Boots," covers the victims with his gun, and takes no chances. But this is all in the play. Pearl has quit the real thing and decided to reform. She will try to elevate the stage instead of robbing it. Pearl is a pretty name, but if those features of hers do not cause a stampede of the audiences when she appears before the foot lights it will be because of her reputation as a dead shot. So that unless someone turns in an alarm of fire, Pearl is pretty sure to hold the audience until the final act.

The fact is, Pearl is an assumed name, as was that of her partners, Joe Boots. When Sheriff Truman of Pinal County arrested the two for stage robbery in 1899, he asked the male highway man his name. He started to answer but only got as far as "Joe," when Pearl supplied the rest - "Boots" and he was tried and convicted and sentenced as Joe Boots. The right name of either one is not known here.

Nearly everyone has read of the stage robbery committed by "Boots" and Pearl Hart. It was in the summer of 1899. The stage between Globe and Riverside was held up, and the passengers robbed of something like four hundred dollars, besides watches and jewelry. One of the victims was the treasurer of Pinal County. There was a Chinaman aboard whom Pearl relieved of over one hundred dollars. The directing spirit of the robbery was Pearl Hart. They were arrested shortly afterwards by Sheriff Ben Truman with considerable plunder still in their possession. They were tried in Florence and on November 18, 1899, Joe Boot was sentenced to thirty years and Pearl Hart to five years in the penitentiary. Boots, strange to say, was made a trusty and escaped after serving less than two years. He has never been found. Pearl's time, according to sentence, would have expired June 16, 1903.

She leaves the prison in good health, and free from the opium habit, to which she was an abject slave on entering the prison. Pearl is a little woman weighing 105 pounds, but she

≈ Frail Prisoners in Yuma Territorial Prison ≈

has the slanging, tough demeanor, and when one contemplates her part in the stage robbery, it must be admitted that she has the nerve, with that facial expression of hers it must be admitted also that she is making further use of her nerve in going before the footlights.

Pearl was not a very desirable prisoner. She took particularly delight in making petty trouble for the other female convicts, and with the least bit of latitude would have made trouble for everyone at the prison, guards, officials, convicts and all, including herself. The women convicts, especially, are doubtless glad she is gone.

Governor Brodie also paroled Rosa Duran last Saturday who was sent from Yavapai County for grand larceny. Her crime consisted of "rolling a man."

Action in both cases was recommended by the Board of Control, the principal reason, perhaps, being on account of the meager accommodations at the prison for women. There are only three female convicts left, and there is really no room for any more."

Pearl Hart died December 30, 1955.

～ Pearl Hart ～

Pearl Hart's Poetry

The sun was brightly shining on a pleasant afternoon
My partner speaking lightly said, "The stage will be here soon."
We saw it coming around the bend and called to them to halt,
And to their pockets we attended, if they got hurt it was their fault.

While the birds were sweetly singing, and the men stood up in line
And the silver softly ringing as it touched this palm of mine.
There we took away their money, but left them enough to eat
And the men looked so funny as they vaulted to their seats.

Then up the road we galloped, quickly through a canyon we did pass
Over the mountains we went swiftly, trying to find our horses grass,
Past the station we boldly went, now along the riverside,
And our horses being spent, of course we had to hide.

In the night we would travel in the daytime try and rest,
And throw ourselves on the gravel, to sleep we would try our best
Around us our horses were stamping looking for some hay or grain
On the road the Posse was tramping, looking for us all in vain.
One more day they would not have got us, but my horse got sore and thin

And my partner was a mean cuss, so Billy Truman roped us in.
Thirty years my partner got, I was given five,
He seemed contented with his lot, and I am still alive.

- Pearl Hart -

In the District Court of the Second Judicial District of the Territory of Arizona,

IN AND FOR THE COUNTY OF PINAL
The Territory of Arizona
    207 vs.   Judgment.
    Pearl H. Art

    The District Attorney W.R. Stone and the defendant in person and by counsel W.M. Griffin and J. M. Morrison came into court and this being the time set for sentence herein, the Court says: "Pearl H. Art stand up.
    On the 7th day of November, A.D. 1899, you were indicted by the Grand Jury of this District for the crime of Robbery.

To this indictment you plead, not guilty. On the 15th day of November, A.D. 1899, you were given a fair and impartial trial, in this court, before a jury of your peers, and said jury returned into open court, their verdict, finding you guilty in manner form as charged in the indictment Have you anything to say or y or legal cause to show why the judgment of this Court should not now be pronounced against you?; The defendant replied nothing. No legal cause being shown or appearing to the Court, the Court doth render its judgment:" That whereas, you Pearl H. Art having been, on the 15th day of November, A.D. 1899, after a fair and impartial trial in this court, found guilty by a jury of your peers, of the crime of Robbery.
    It is Ordered, Adjudged and Decreed that you, Pearl Hart, are guilty of the crime of Robbery and that you be punished therefor by imprisonment in the Territorial Prison at Yuma, Arizona for the term of five years commencing from the date of sentence herein, viz: the 17th day of November, A.D. 1899.
    And it is further Ordered that you be, and you are hereby remanded to the custody of the Sheriff of Pimal County, Arizona, to be by him, safely delivered into the custody of the proper officers of said Territorial prison.

      District Court
Of the Second Judicial District
    Territory of Arizona

In and for Pinal County
    I, Daniel C. Stevens, Clerk of the District Court of the Second Judicial District of the Territory of Arizona, in and for Pinal County do hereby certify the foregoing to be a full, true and correct copy of the Judgment duly made and entered on the Minutes of the said District Court in the above entitled action, and that I have compared the same with the original, that the same is a correct transcript therefrom and of the whole thereof.
    Attest my hand and the seal of the said District Court this 17th day of November 1899
        Daniel C. Stevens   Clerk
  By   Gilbert T. Colton   Deputy Clerk

~ Pearl Hart ~

TERRITORIAL PRISON AT YUMA, A.T.

Description of Convict

NAME:
    Pearl Hart
ALIAS:

CRIME:
    Robbery
COUNTY:
    Pinal
LEGITIMATE OCCUPATION:
    None
HABITS:
    Intemperate
OPIUM:
    Morphine
HEIGHT:
    5' 3"
SIZE OF HEAD:
    Black
COLOR EYES:
    Gray
MARRIED:
    Yes
CAN READ:
Yes
WHERE EDUCATED:
    United States

NUMBER:
    1559
SENTENCE:
    5 yrs. from
    Nov. 17, 1899
NATIVITY:
    Canada
AGE:
    28
TOBACCO:
    Yes
RELIGION:
    Catholic
SIZE FOOT:
    2-1/2
WEIGHT:
    100 lbs.
COLOR HAIR:

CHILDREN:
    2
CAN WRITE:
    Yes
FORMER IMPRISONMENT:

NEAREST RELATIVE:
    Mother
    Mrs. James Taylor, Jr.
    (Relative)

WHEN AND HOW DISCHARGED:
    Dec. 15, 1902, Paroled by Gov. Brodie

PRISON RECORD

Complexion - Med. Dark

~ Frail Prisoners in Yuma Territorial Prison ~

Elena Estrada

Chapter 14

Elena Estrada ~ No. 1685

The Arizona Daily Citizen, July 5, 1900, related:

> "Last night about 8:30 o'clock Alena [sic] Estrada wound up her fourth of July celebration in an alley by stabbing Rufugio Bindiola. The cut, which is in the abdomen, is likely to prove serious."

Actually, the location of the stabbing was Gay Alley and the wound was serious. Bindiola, a native of Sonora, Mexico, was carried to the nearby home of a friend across the railroad tracks where he died soon after.

Estrada was taken before Justice of the Peace William Scott, on a misdemeanor charge and was sentenced to the county jail for 100 days. Here she will remain until the district attorney decides the proper action he will pursue.

On July 6, 1900, a coroner's jury met in Justice Scott's office and investigated the incident. They came to the conclusion that Bindiola came to his death from a knife wound inflicted by Elena Estrada. Evidently, the entire episode was caused by drunkenness as there is no evidence that a quarrel or disagreement took place before the stabbing.

L.W. Wakefield appeared before Justice Scott on July 7, 1900, and swore out a complaint that Elena Estrada did willfully, unlawfully, feloniously, deliberately, premeditatedly, and of her malice aforethought, stab, strike, wound, kill, and murder one Rufugio Bindiola.

~ Frail Prisoners in Yuma Territorial Prison ~

Justice Scott arraigned Estrada and held her for examination without bail on July 9, 1900. The Grand Jury indicted her for the murder of Rufugio Bindiola on October 1, 1900.

During her trial Estrada's story was that she was holding a knife in her hand and Bindiola fell against it, inflicting the wound in his abdomen and ultimately causing his death. It is evident that her testimony was not believed as she was found guilty of manslaughter and sentenced to the Territorial Prison for 7 years, beginning on October 20, 1900.

When Elena arrived at Yuma the only other woman incarcerated there was Pearl Hart. It was likely that the two women did not get along, but they kept their disagreements from becoming physical.

Estrada's records show that she was locked in the dark cell five days for fighting on September 15, 1902. The only other prisoner whose record correlates with that of Estrada is Rose Duran, who was also put in the dark cell for five days for fighting on September 15, 1902. It is obvious that these two frail prisoners tangled. Duran had arrived at the prison on November 15, 1901.

Elena Estrada served four years and one month of her seven years sentence. She was paroled by acting Governor Nichols on November 26, 1904. Most likely this parole was granted for the convenience of the politicians and prison officials.

The Graham Guardian, December 2, 1904, carried a last report on Estrada:

"NO WOMEN LEFT

The Last Female Prisoner Released From Yuma

Acting Governor Nichols yesterday granted a parole to Elena Estrada, who was serving a seven years term in the penitentiary for manslaughter, having been sentenced from Pima County. For some time she has been the only female inmate of the penitentiary and perhaps that fact had something to do with the granting of the parole. But, at any rate she would not

~ Elena Estrada ~

have had much longer to serve for her time with allowance for good conduct would expire next summer.

Her crime was the killing of a man from Tucson. She was a member of the underworld and had a lover who was somewhat mixed up with her in the death of her victim, but he could not directly be connected with the case."

In the Justice Court

First Precinct, County of Pima Territory of Arizona.
The Territory of Arizona, Plaintiff.
        vs.   Complaint-Criminal
Elena Estrada

Personally appeared before me, this 7th day of July, 1900 L.W. Wakefield who, being first duly sworn, complains and says: That one Elena Estrada, on or about the 4th day of July 1900, at Tucson, First Precinct, County and Territory aforesaid, committed a Murder as follows, to wit: the said Elena Estrada did, at the time and place aforesaid, willfully, unlawfully, feloniously, deliberately, premeditatedly, and of her malice aforethought, stab, strike, wound, kill and murder one Refugio Bindiola, then and there being,

All of which is contrary to the form of the Statute in such case made and provided, and against the peace and dignity of the Territory of Arizona.
                  L.W. Wakefield
Subscribed and sworn to before me this 7th day of July 1900
                  Wm. F. Scott
                  Justice of the Peace of said Precinct

Frail Prisoners in Yuma Territorial Prison

IN THE DISTRICT COURT
Of the First Judicial District
Territory of Arizona, in and for Yuma County

The Territory of Arizona, Plaintiff
vs. **INDICTMENT**
Elena Estrada, Defendant

October Term, A.D. 1900

Elena Estrada is accused by the Grand Jury of Pima County, Territory of Arizona, by this Indictment, found on the 1st day of October A.D. 1900 of the crime of Murder, committed as follows, to wit: The said Elena Estrada on or about the 4th day of July A.D. 1900 and before the finding of this Indictment, at the County of Pima, Territory of Arizona did then and there unlawfully, feloniously, willfully, deliberately, premeditatedly, and of her malice aforethought, assault, strike, stab, wound, kill and murder one Refugio Bindiola, then and there being contrary to the form, force and effect of the Statute in such cases made and provided and against the peace and dignity of the Territory of Arizona.

William F. Cooper
District Attorney

~ Elena Estrada ~

TERRITORIAL PRISON AT YUMA, A.T.

Description of Convict

NAME:
    Elena Estrada
ALIAS:

CRIME:
    Manslaughter
COUNTY:
    Pima
LEGITIMATE OCCUPATION:
    (None listed)
HABITS:
    Temperate
OPIUM:
    No
HEIGHT:
    5' 10"
SIZE OF HEAD:
    Black
COLOR EYES:
    Black
MARRIED:
    No
CAN READ:
    Yes
WHERE EDUCATED:
    Mexico (Public)

NUMBER:
    1685
SENTENCE:
    7 yrs. from
    Oct. 20, 1900
NATIVITY:
    Mexico
AGE:
    25
TOBACCO
    Yes
RELIGION:
    Catholic
SIZE FOOT:
    5
WEIGHT:
    129 lbs.
COLOR HAIR:

CHILDREN:

CAN WRITE:
    Yes
FORMER IMPRISONMENT:

NEAREST RELATIVE:
    Has parents - Mother

WHEN AND HOW DISCHARGED:
    Nov. 26, 1904   Paroled by Acting Gov. Nickols

PRISON RECORD

Condition of teeth - Good
Sept. 15, 1902 - Dark cell   five days for fighting

Frail Prisoners in Yuma Territorial Prison

Alfrida Mercer

Alfrida Mercer~No. 1816

A complaint was filed against Alfrida Mercer on October 31, 1900, in the Third Judicial District of the Territory of Arizona and Maricopa County. Her crime was described as being a married woman, who did unlawfully, willfully, and feloniously have carnal knowledge of the body of Frederick Crosley, a man who was not her husband.

Alfrida and Crosley were charged with violating the Edmond's Act or in simple language--adultery. When they were arraigned her bail was set at $100. The court decided to try them separately and Alfrida was indicted on November 10, 1900. At that time her bail was set at $500.

She entered a plea of not guilty and her lawyer, Tom Flannigan, had her bail reduced to $250. During her trial a number of witnesses appeared against her: Mrs. Belle Crosley (wife of Frederick), J.R. Encinas, O.C. Smith, Andrew Nielson, and her cohort in the crime, Frederick Crosley.

Author's note: This writer can not help but wonder what testimony these witnesses (other than Fred Crosley) for the prosecution gave. Unless they were actual eye witnesses, their testimony could only be supposition.

Needless to say, Alfrida was found guilty and sentenced to six months in the Territorial Prison, her term starting from November 15, 1901. She was released after five months on April 14, 1902.

⚘ Frail Prisoners in Yuma Territorial Prison ⚘

Court Record - Alfrida Mercer

INDICTMENT: No. 532

IN THE DISTRICT COURT OF THE Third JUDICIAL DISTRICT OF THE TERRITORY OF ARIZONA

Having and exercising the same jurisdiction in all cases arising under the constitution and laws of the United States as is vested in the Circuit and District Courts of the United States.

UNITED STATES of AMERICA   In the District Court of the 3rd
   vs.   Judicial District of the Territory
Alfrida Mercer   of Arizona, the 10th day of November one thousand nine hundred.

Alfrida Mercer is accused by the Grand Jury of the United States, chosen selected, and sworn within the and for the 3rd Judicial District of the Territory of Arizona, in the name and by the authority
United States of America, by this indictment, of the crime of
Adultery, committed as follows: That the said Alfrida Mercer late of the 3rd Judicial District of the Territory of Arizona, and within the county of Maricopa in said Territory of Arizona then and there being a married woman did unlawfully, willfully and feloniously have carnal knowledge of the body of one Frederick Crosley, a man, he the said Frederick Crosley then and there not being the husband of her the said Alfrida Mercer.

And so the Grand Jurors aforesaid, upon their oaths aforesaid, do say that the said Alfrida Mercer in the manner and form aforesaid, and at the time and place aforesaid, did then and there commit the Crime of Adultery contrary to the form of the statute in such case made and provided, and against the peace and dignity of the United States of America.

   Robert E. Morrison
   United States Attorney for the
   Territory of Arizona.

Presented to the Court in the presence of the Grand Jury by their Foreman, and filed this 10th day of November 1900.
   W.C. Foster
   Clerk
Witnesses examined before the Grand Jury on the finding of this Indictment: Mrs. Belle Crosley, Andrew Neilson, J.R. Encinas,
   O.C. Smith, Frederick Crosley, T.D. Bennett.

~ Alfrida Mercer ~

Court Record - Alfrida Mercer

Court Docket

Criminal Register of Actions, United States District Court 3rd District

The United States No. 527	R.E. Morrison, U.S. Attorney
vs	Thos. D. Bennett
Alfrida Mercer	Ass't U.S. Attorney

Frederick Crosley

1900

Oct. 31 Filed Complaint (2)   Adultery, held to answer
         Filed Warrant Arrest   Alfrida Mercer, Released on
         bail $100
         Filed Subpoena
         Filed Mittimus (temporary)   Nov. 10/1900 Alfrida Mercer
         indicted for Adultery.
         Filed Bond Mrs. Mercer
         $100   Nov. 10/1900, Frederick Crosley
         indicted for Adultery.

         Filed Mittimus (final)

Nov. 9 Entered order of Court, appointing Geo. D. Christy, Atty
         for Crosley before Grand Jury.
Upon finding of the Indictment this case separated, and re-entered as Case Nos. 532 and 533.

Nov. 10 Filed indictment
         Entered Order for Bench Warrant
         Entered Order fixing Bail $500.
         Entered Order to appear for arraignment, Nov. 15/1900 9:30 a.m.

     13 Filed Warranty on Rtn (sic)
         Entering Rtn U.S.M., "Warranty served on Nov. 10/1900,
         on deft. and body now in custody. Wm. M. Griffith
                                     by J.A. Portinis, (sic) Dep."

     15 Entered arraignment and Plea of "Not Guilty."
         Copy of indictment of deft.
         Certificate to copy.
         Order setting trial Dec. 19/1900
         Order reducing bail to $250.

✺ Frail Prisoners in Yuma Territorial Prison ✺

    20 Drawing recognizance
         Filed & approved Bond, $250.

Dec. 3   Order for Bench Warrant and discharge of bail.
        Issued Bench Warrant

     4   Filed Warranty on return
        Entered Rtn of U.S.M., "Warranty served upon deft. Dec. 4/1900, and body now in custody. W.M. Griffith, U.S.M.
                       by J.A. Pontenis Dep. U.S.M.
                       Dated Dec. 4th 1900

     4   Issued Commitment

                          Copy of Commitment

1816 — Alfrida Mercer

PRISON RECORD

Complexion - Dark
Fred Crossley, #1713 testified at her trial.
Arizona Sentinel   Nov. 1901

    Mrs. Alfrida Mercer, who was convicted and sentenced to six months confinement in the Territorial Prison at the last term of U.S. Courts at Phoenix for violating the Edmonds Act, was brought down by Deputy Marshall Wells last Saturday. Mrs. Mercer is the mother of several children, and strange, to say, her husband stood by her to the last.

Alfrida Mercer

TERRITORIAL PRISON AT YUMA, A.T.

Description of Convict

NAME: Alfrida Mercer
NUMBER: 1816
ALIAS:
SENTENCE: 6 mos. from Nov. 15, 1901
CRIME: Adultery
NATIVITY: Pennsylvania
COUNTY: Maricopa
AGE: 37
LEGITIMATE OCCUPATION: None
TOBACCO: No
HABITS: Temperate
RELIGION: Protestant
OPIUM: No
SIZE FOOT: 2-1/2
HEIGHT: 4' 11'1/2"
WEIGHT: 110 lbs.
SIZE OF HEAD:
COLOR HAIR: Black
COLOR EYES: Brown
CHILDREN: Two
MARRIED: Yes
CAN WRITE: Yes
CAN READ: Yes
FORMER IMPRISONMENT:
WHERE EDUCATED: Pennsylvania
NEAREST RELATIVE: No parents
Nearest relative: Stephen Mercer Phoenix, Az. (husband) (Relative)

WHEN AND HOW DISCHARGED: April 14, 1902, Expiration of Sentence

❦ Frail Prisoners in Yuma Territorial Prison ❦

Main Guard Station

Chapter 16
Rosa Duran~No. 1818

Rosa was charged with grand larceny on November 9, 1901 and entered a plea of not guilty. The grand jury indicted her and her trial was set for November 14, 1901.

Her crime was committed at Ash Fork, Arizona and even though she was only 16, the court took no notice of her young age or her plea of not guilty. They found her guilty of grand larceny and sentenced her to three years in the Territorial Prison, her sentence to begin on November 15, 1901.

Fortune finally smiled on Rosa, however, as by 1902 the prison was becoming overcrowded at an alarming rate. The superintendent recommended Rosa for parole because of the crowded conditions in the women's ward. Governor Brodie granted that parole on December 15, 1902. Rosa Duran had served only 13 months of her three years sentence.

☙ Frail Prisoners in Yuma Territorial Prison ☙

Arizona Daily Journal   Miner November 9, 1901

DISTRICT COURT PROCEEDINGS:
(In part)

Saturday, Nov. 9 - The grand jury yesterday afternoon returned six indictments for embezzlement against Fred Guimond of Jerome.

Territory vs. Manuel Aranda et al; demurrer overruled and plea of not guilty entered. J.H. Wright was entered as counsel for Pomesius Chavez and the attorney of Leopold Aranda asked for a separate trial, which was granted.

Rosa Duran and Thomas Powlas plead not guilty and their trials were set for Nov. 14.

H.P. Torber, who plead guilty to a charge of burglary, was sentenced to the Territorial Prison for two years and six months, dated from the time of his arrest.

Grand Jury reported indictments as follows: Lee Townsend, murder; Frank McMurrain, two indictments, burglary; Geo. Roop, assault with deadly weapon.

Guimond, Roop and McMurrain each entered a plea of not guilty this afternoon.

November 14, 1901
Rosa Duran was yesterday found guilty of grand larceny by a jury. The crime was committed at Ash Fork.

November 18, 1901
Sheriff Munds left last night for Yuma with Rosa Duran and H.P. Fauber, the former under a three years sentence for robbery committed at Ash Fork and the latter for two years and six months for burglary.

Recommended for parole by the Superintendent because of the crowded conditions in the women's ward. Paroled Dec. 15, 1902.

Was living in Prescott when she reported from parole March 7, 1903, June 10, 1903, December 29, 1903. Time expired March 14, 1904.

Arizona Daily Journal-Miner

November 9, 1901
Rosa Daron (sic) plead not guilty and trial was set for Nov. 14.
                                        - In the District Court Proceedings

November 14, 1901
Rosa Daron (sic) was yesterday found guilty of grand larceny by a jury. The crime was committed at Ash Fork.

November 18, 1901
Sheriff Munds left last night for Yuma with Rosa Daron (sic) and H.P. Fauber, the former under a three years sentence for robbery committed at Ash Fork and the latter for two years and six months for burglary.

~ Rosa Duran ~

TERRITORIAL PRISON AT YUMA, A.T.

Description of Convict

NAME:
  Rosa Duran
ALIAS:

CRIME:
  Grand Larceny
COUNTY:
  Yavapai
LEGITIMATE OCCUPATION:
  None
HABITS:
  Temperate
OPIUM:
  No
HEIGHT:
  4' 11"
SIZE OF HEAD:

COLOR EYES:
  Black
MARRIED:
  No
CAN READ:
  No
WHERE EDUCATED:
  United States

NUMBER:
  1818
SENTENCE:
  3 yrs. from
  Nov. 15, 1901
NATIVITY:
  Mexico
AGE:
  16
TOBACCO:
  Yes
RELIGION:
  Catholic
SIZE FOOT:
  3-1/2
WEIGHT:
  116 lbs.
COLOR HAIR:
  Black
CHILDREN:

CAN WRITE:
  No
FORMER IMPRISONMENT:

NEAREST RELATIVE:
  Juliano Almendex,
  Williams, Az.

WHEN AND HOW DISCHARGED:
  Dec. 15, 1902, Paroled by Gov. Brodie
  Brought in by Sheriff Munda

PRISON RECORD

Complexion - Med. Dark   Teeth - bad
Sept. 15, 1902 - Dark cell   3 days for fighting

☞ **Frail Prisoners in Yuma Territorial Prison** ☜

Bertha Trimble

Chapter 17

Bertha Trimble~No. 1919

Walter and Bertha Trimble were charged with most repulsive crimes. Walter was charged with the rape of Bertha's daughter, Lydia Sparks, who was a twelve year old child. Bertha was charged with holding her daughter while Walter committed the rape.

At a later date, the girl told the story of a gruesome murder that was committed in New Mexico and the victim's body being buried on the banks of the Pecos River. The Trimbles and Lydia had drifted on to Graham County, Arizona. The rape occurred in Duncan.

Shortly after, the Trimbles became frightened that their past was catching up to them. They fled to old Mexico, abandoning Lydia. Constable Hill and his wife took the child into their home.

Lydia was so frightened and distrustful that it was some time before she would tell the Hills about the assault by Trimble. They promised to protect her and she gave the full particulars of a most outrageous crime. When this little girl told them of her treatment at the hands of the Trimbles, they sent for District Attorney Leo Stratton and Graham County Sheriff "Hard-Times" Parks to hear this story. They went to work on the case at once.

In February, 1902, Captain Burt Mossman of the Arizona Rangers, located and arrested Walter and Bertha Trimble in Cananea, Sonora, Mexico. District Attorney Stratton had already secured all the papers that were necessary and Mossman brought them back to Bisbee, Arizona. Sheriff Parks was wired to come get them.

❦ Frail Prisoners in Yuma Territorial Prison ❧

When Parks arrived in Bisbee, he found Walter in the local jail--but Bertha had taken lodging in the town. Parks immediately placed her under arrest and departed for Solomonville with the two prisoners.

The Copper Era, February 27, 1902, wrote: "Trimble is charged with assault upon the person of the alleged daughter of his wife, a mere child of ten or twelve years. Mrs. Trimble was a participant in the crime using force against the girl, which leads many to believe that she is not the child's mother. The crime was committed at Duncan last summer, and is of such a revolting nature that the details cannot be given to the public."

The Arizona Sentinel, October 20, 1902, reported:

"One can almost believe in total depravity after reading the proceedings of the trial of Trimble, the rapist, who outraged his little 12 year old stepdaughter, her mother assisting in the revolting crime, by holding the child while the fiend accomplished his purpose."

Both Walter and Bertha were charged with the crime of rape. Up until that time no woman had ever been charged with rape in Arizona Territory.

The Arizona Silver Belt, March 6, 1902, declared:

"Feeling is very bitter in Graham County over the affair, and Trimble did not escape any too quick to prevent a lynching bee."

On October 24, 1902, the Arizona Bulletin reported on the trial:

"AN AWFUL CHARGE: The jury in the case of the Territory vs. Bettie (sic) Trimble, after being out but a few minutes Tuesday evening, returned into court with a verdict of aiding the (sic) abetting her husband, Walter Trimble, in the accomplishment of a most heinous crime on the person of her own daughter by a former husband.

The charges in this case were of a most repulsive character and has been a shock to the decency of the entire community. The defendant was represented by Judge McFarland and all the skill and ingenuity of a veteran lawyer was invoked in her behalf, and some unexpected phases of the case were developed by the defense, but all to no avail.

It is to be hoped that the criminal records of Graham County will never be polluted again with cases of the nature and repulsiveness of the charges against the Trimbles."

Both Walter and Bertha were found guilty as charged and sentenced to the Territorial Prison for life. The newspapers commented that the penalty was utterly inadequate for the crime.

Though confined behind the adobe and stone walls at Yuma, Bertha managed to get a plan for her release from prison to her sister, a Mrs. Hayes. The plan was for this Mrs. Hayes to kidnap Lydia Sparks and force her to refute her testimony. But, Lydia was nowhere to be found. Prosecutor Rawlings and his wife had made sure of that. In fact, Mrs. Rawlings had taken the child to Los Angeles.

However, some busybody told Mrs. Hayes where Lydia was and she went to their hotel in Los Angeles. She spent eight days with Lydia and Mrs. Rawlings using an assumed name. She hired another woman who posed as a nurse, and in this guise attached herself to the woman and little girl. As a friendly gesture she suggested that she be allowed to take Lydia to the beach and other places of amusement.

Mrs. Hayes already had depositions made out for Lydia to sign, swearing that the testimony she had given at the trial was false. Once she had signed these, Lydia was to be taken to San Francisco where she would conveniently disappear. Rawlings, ever suspicious, spoiled Hayes' plans by having the police take his wife and Lydia into protective custody.

Mrs. Hayes did manage to secure Bertha a new trial. Bertha's attorney, Juluis Baker of Phoenix, made application for a change of venue, pleading the excited state of local public sentiment against his client in Graham County. Judge Doan had no choice but to agree. Even if the new trial was held in another, Graham County was still obliged to pay the costs.

When Judge Doan started the order for the change, District Attorney Rawlings stopped him. With obvious reluctance he explained to the court that the first trial had been long and most expensive. The county treasury would not be able to afford another such trial. Therefore, he had to move for a dismissal of the charges on Bertha Trimble on the grounds that Graham County could not bear the expense of another trial. Besides--the Arizona Statutes had no crime such as accessory to the crime of rape.

Part of the conditions of the dismissal were that Bertha would leave the Territory of Arizona and never return. She agreed and was placed on a train--some say to Mexico--some say to California. Bertha spent one year and eight months in jails and the Territorial Prison. She was released by order of the Supreme Court of Arizona, April 21, 1903.

Walter appealed his case to the Supreme Court, but it was dismissed. After serving almost four years, Walter Trimble was pardoned.

Arizona Sentinel   **October 20, 1902**

One can almost believe in total depravity after reading the proceedings of the trial of Trimble, the rapist, who outraged his little 12-year-old stepdaughter, her mother assisting in the revolting crime, by holding the child while the fiend accomplished his purpose. He was sentenced to the penitentiary for life--the penalty being utterly inadequate for the crime. The woman received the same sentence and both were lodged in the prison last Sunday morning. The crime was committed in Graham County where the Trimbles were living.

The Graham Guardian   **October 30, 1903**

From District Court: The rape case of Bettie (sic) Trimble was dismissed on Saturday with the understanding that she must go to Mexico and remain there. The defense in this case was determined to get a change of venue in the case, which would have been a very expensive proposition for the county, and in view of the fact that she has already served six months in the penitentiary and a year and a half in the county jail, and in view of the fact that she was only charged as an accomplice and that the principal in the case will probably never again see outside the walls of the penitentiary, it was thought wise to dismiss her.

The Arizona Bulletin   October 30, 1903

BERTHA TRIMBLE FREE: Bertha Trimble, who has been an inmate of the county jail for nearly two years, was given her liberty Monday afternoon. The offense with which she was charged, and on which she was at one time convicted and sentenced to the penitentiary for life, is too revolting and too well known in Graham County to need repeating. Suffice it is to say that her crime was almost inhuman. Tuesday afternoon Mrs. Trimble was an outgoing passenger on the train bound for Old Mexico where she will probably remain and attempt to live down the disgrace of a prison record. The case against her was dismissed on motion of District Attorney Rawlings.

> The Arizona Bulletin, November 24, 1905, wrote:
> "There is a governor in Arizona to pardon rapists as soon as the prison walls claim them, especially if the fiend has a fair sister with a shady reputation to mediate for him."

Frail Prisoners in Yuma Territorial Prison

TERRITORIAL PRISON AT YUMA, A.T.

Description of Convict

NAME:
  Bertha Trimble
ALIAS:
  Natural Life from
CRIME:
  Rape
COUNTY:
  Graham
LEGITIMATE OCCUPATION:
  Housewife
HABITS:
  Intemperate
OPIUM:
  5
HEIGHT:
  5' 3"
SIZE OF HEAD:
  Brown
COLOR EYES:
  Brown
MARRIED:
  Yes
CAN READ:
  Yes
WHERE EDUCATED:
Texas

NUMBER:
  1919
SENTENCE
  Oct., 1902
NATIVITY:
  Texas
AGE:
  37
TOBACCO:

RELIGION:
  Protestant
SIZE FOOT:

WEIGHT:
  200 lbs.
COLOR HAIR:

CHILDREN:
  3
CAN WRITE:
  Yes
FORMER IMPRISONMENT

NEAREST RELATIVE:
No Parents
Son,   Agua Caliente,
Chihuahua, Mexico

WHEN AND HOW DISCHARGED:
  Discharged by Order of Supreme Court of Arizona, April   21, 1903

PRISON RECORD

Arrested by Arizona Rangers, 2-22-02 at La Cananea, Mexico
Forehead - Medium   Carriage - erect   Teeth - Fair
Physical peculiarities; Mole on left side chin, mole on right side upper lip, mole on inside corner of both eyes, 2 moles on right cheek; 1 below left ear; six brown moles supper back; one brown mole high on left shoulder; one brown mole on right front collarbone; No examination for further marks made.

Chapter 18

Jesus Chacon ~ No. 1933

Taken from Report of Superintendent - December 31, 1902

"Health of Prisoners:

The case of smallpox was confined to the female department of the prison, the infected person being Jesus Chacon, No. 1933, a female prisoner sent here from Solomonville on November 9th, last. Three days after her arrival she broke out, and which development was our first warning of the disease. Prompt and heroic measures were at once enforced to prevent a spread of the dread disease. Another female prisoner, at her own suggestion, had charge of the case as nurse, and administered, very successfully, to the wants of the patient under instructions of the physician."

Chacon served ten months of her twelve months sentence, being discharged on August 26, 1903.

❦ Frail Prisoners in Yuma Territorial Prison ❦

TERRITORIAL PRISON AT YUMA, A.T.

Description of Convict

NAME:
  Jesus Chacon
ALIAS:

CRIME:
  Arson
COUNTY:
  Graham
LEGITIMATE OCCUPATION:
  Seamstress
HABITS:
  Temperate
OPIUM:
  Morphine
HEIGHT:
4' 11-3/4"
SIZE OF HEAD:

COLOR EYES:
  Black
MARRIED:
  No
CAN READ:
Yes
WHERE EDUCATED:

NUMBER:
  1933
SENTENCE:
  1 yr. from
  Oct. 27, 1902
NATIVITY:
  Arizona
AGE:
  19
TOBACCO:
  Yes
RELIGION:
  Catholic
SIZE FOOT:
  5-1/2
WEIGHT:
  130 lbs.
COLOR HAIR:
  Black
CHILDREN:
  2
CAN WRITE:
  Yes
FORMER IMPRISONMENT:

NEAREST RELATIVE
  Mother
  Mrs. Casimera Villa
  Tucson, Arizona

WHEN AND HOW DISCHARGED:
  Aug. 26, 1903, Expiration of Sentence

PRISON RECORD

Carriage - erect   Teeth - Good   Forehead - Low
Scars: Scar on forehead - 1-1/2 inches inside of left eye, scar on top of shoulder, scar on back and right side of neck, scar on front of left forearm.

   The Arizona Bulletin - July 11, 1902 - Jesus Chacon, an eighteen year old girl was brought to the county jail this week from Morenci to be held to the grand jury on the charge of burning a house.

Chapter 19

Kate Nelson~No. 2219

On December 13, 1904, the Grand Jury of the United States of America indicted B.W. Birch and Kate Nelson for the crime of adultery: On November 19, 1904, in the County of Cochise, the two did unlawfully and willfully have carnal knowledge each of the body of the other, Kate Nelson being a married woman, having a husband in full life and B.W. Birch being a married man not her husband.

And so the Grand Jurors aforesaid upon their oaths, aforesaid, do say that the said B.W. Birch and Kate Nelson in the manner and form aforesaid, and at the time and place aforesaid, did then and there commit the crime of adultery, contrary to the form of the statue in such case, made and provided, and against the peace and dignity of the United States of America.

The defendants were ordered to answer to the indictment December 14, 1904. Both entered a plea of not guilty and their case was set for trial the following day.

The following witnesses were called by the prosecution: Mrs. Charles Fetterly, Mrs. Mary Younghause, W. Kline, Mr. Coffey, Ole Nelson, E.R. Pritle, F.W. Hill, J.M. Durnal, and F.M. Pierronnet. When these witnesses had completed their testimony, the prosecution rested its case.

Author's note: Again this writer is appalled at the number of witnesses to an act of adultery.

The defense called Kate Nelson, B.W. Birch, and Mr. Soderman. After their testimony there was no further evidence to be heard so the defense rested.

As expected, the Jury found both defendants guilty as charged in the indictment. Both were sentenced to two years at hard labor in the Territorial Prison at Yuma, Arizona.

Kate served 19 months of her 24 months sentence and was discharged on July 19, 1906.

Court Records - Kate Nelson

Dec. 13, 1904: In the District Court of the Second Judicial District of the Territory of Arizona. Having and exercising the same jurisdiction in all cases arising under the Constitution and laws of the United States as is vested in the Circuit and District Courts of the United States.

603   United States of America
vs   **Indictment**
B.W. Birch and Kate Nelson

In the District Court of the Second Judicial District of the Territory of Arizona, the Thirteenth day of December, One thousand nine hundred and Four. B.W. Birch and Kate Nelson are accused by the Grand Jury of the United States of America, chosen, selected and sworn within and for the Second Judicial District of the Territory of Arizona. In the names and by the authority of the United States of America, by this indictment of the crime of Adultery, committed as follows: That the said B.W.

Kate Nelson

Birch and Kate Nelson late of the Second Judicial District aforesaid, to wit: On the nineteenth day of November, A.D. 1904, One Thousand nine hundred and four, and within the said second Judicial District of the Territory of Arizona did unlawfully and willfully have carnal knowledge each of the body of the other, the said Kate Nelson then and there being a married woman, having then and there being a married woman, having then and there a husband in full life and he, the said B.W. Birch, then and there being a man not her husband. And so the Grand Jurors aforesaid upon their oaths, aforesaid, do say that the Said B.W. Birch and Kate Nelson in the manner and form aforesaid, and at the time and place aforesaid, did then and there commit the crime of Adultery; contrary to the form of the statute in such case (sic) made and provided, and against the peace and dignity of the United States of America

Frederick S. Nave
United States Attorney for the Territory of Arizona
No. 603In the District Court, 2nd Judicial District

J.F. Niccolls, Foreman of the Grand Jury. Mrs. Charels Fetterly, Mrs. Mary Younghans, E.R. Pirtle, J.M. Durnal, W. Kline. Presented to the Court, in the presence of the Grand Jury by their Foreman, and filed this 13th day of December, 1904.

Geo. B. Wilcox, Clerk

The United States
vs.   Arraignment
B.W. Birch and Kate Nelson

The United States Attorney, the defendant in person and by counsel came into open Court and said defendants were duly arraigned by the Clerk reading to them the indictment herein and at the same time and by order of the Court handing to them a true copy of the indictment, the defendants upon being interrogated by the Court, state that their true names are as set out in the indictment. It is by the Court ordered that defendants appear and answer to the indictment herein tomorrow, Dec. 14th, at 9 o'clock a.m. The defendants were thereupon remanded to the custody of the U.S. Marshal.

The United States
vs.   Plea
B.W. Birch and Kate Nelson

The District Attorney being present comes now the defendant in person and with their counsel into open Court and this being the time set for the defendant to plead to the indictment herein, defendants enter a plea of "Not Guilty" whereupon it is by the Court ordered that this case be set for trial Dec. 15th, at 9 o'clock p.m. Whereupon the defendants were remanded to the custody of the United States Marshal.

Dec. 15, 1904

The United States
vs.   Trial No. 603
B.W. Birch and Kate Nelson

The United States Attorney being present comes not the defendant herein in person and with their counsel J.F. Ross, esq. into open Court and both parties announce ready for trial, whereupon the Clerk was ordered to draw twenty names from the Box, wherein he had deposited in the presence of the Court, the names of the jurors summoned and not excused, and the names of twenty persons were thereupon drawn, and all answering to their names, took their places in the jury box. The Jurors were then sworn and examined on their voir dire. The panel being now full and complete and said Jurors in the Jury Box, being passed for cause by both parties, the respective parties having exercised their right of peremptory challenges, the following persons were called according to law to constitute the jury viz: O.P. Hunt, Oscar E. Reynolds, H. Bradley, D.W. Hawk (sic) J.B. Besner, John McGill, A.M. St. Clair, L. McCord, J.E. Mays, Albert Wittig, J.W. Dunningan and E.O. Devine who were duly sworn to well and truly try the issue joined between the United States of America and the defendants herein, thereupon the Clerk read aloud to the jury the indictment herein and stated the plea of the defendant thereto, to wit: "Not Guilty" which is the issue to be tried herein. And the prosecution to maintain upon its part the issues herein called as witnesses the following named persons, to wit: Mrs. Chas. Fetterly, Mrs. Mary Younghause, F.M. Pierronnet, J.M. Durnal, F.W. Hill, E.R. Pritle, Ole Nelson, Mr. Coffey and W. Kline, who were sworn, examined and cross examined, whereupon the prosecution rested its case. Comes now the Counsel for the defendant and moves the Court to instruct the Jury to acquit, which motion was by the Court denied. Whereupon the Counsel for the defendants to maintain upon their part the issues herein, calls as witnesses the following named persons to wit: Mr. Soderman, Mrs. Kate Nelson and B.W. Birch, who were duly sworn, examined and cross-examined. There being no further evidence to be heard the defense rests. Argument of the respective counsel followed the instructions of the Court. The said cause being now fully submitted, the Said Jury retire in charge of their Bailiff James Mulligan, an officer of this Court first duly sworn for that purpose to consider of their verdict. And subsequently said Jury return into open Court their names being called and all answering thereto respectively, being asked if they had agreed upon a verdict, thru their Foreman, reply that they have and thereupon thru their foreman, present the verdict as follows, to wit:

❧ Frail Prisoners in Yuma Territorial Prison ❧

No. 603 - Verdict
The United States
vs
B.W. Birch and Mrs. Kate Nelson
Defendants

We, The jury duly empanelled and sworn in the above entitled cause, upon our oaths do find the defendants guilty as charged in the indictment.

John McGill, Foreman

And the said Jury being interrogated by the Court say that this is their verdict and so say they all. Whereupon the Court ordered the said verdict recorded, and said jury discharged from the case. The defendants were thereupon remanded to the custody of the U.S. Marshal, to appear for sentence and Judgement at 9 o'clock a.m.
Dec. 16th, 1904

Sentence   603   December 16, 1904

The United States
vs.
B.W. Birch

The defendant being present in open Court in person and by his counsel J.F. Ross, the United States Attorney for Arizona present on the part of the United States, and this being the time heretofore fixed for passing Judgment on the defendant in this case. The defendant B.W. Birch was duly informed by the Court of the nature of the indictment found against him for the crime of Adultery committed on the 19th day of Nov. A.D. 1904, of his arraignment and plea of "Not Guilty" as charged in the indictment of the trial and the verdict of the Jury on the 15th day of December A.D. 1904. Guilty as charged in the indictment. The defendant was then asked if he had any legal cause to show why judgment should not be pronounced against him. And no sufficient cause being shown or appearing to the Court, thereupon the Court renders its judgment. That, whereas you, B.W. Birch, having been duly convicted in this Court of the crime of Adultery, it is found by the Court that you are so guilty of the said crime. It is therefore Ordered, Adjudged and Decreed and the judgment and sentence of the Court is, that you B.W. Birch be punished by imprisonment, in the Territorial Prison at Yuma, Arizona at hard labor for a term of two (2) years, to date from Dec. 16, 1904. The defendant was then remanded to the custody of the U.S. Marshal for said Arizona Territory, to be by him delivered into the custody of the proper officers of said Territorial Prison at Yuma, Arizona. And It Is Further Ordered, that a certified copy of this Judgment shall be a sufficient Warrant for the said Marshal to take, keep and safely deliver the said B.W. Birch into the custody of the proper officers, of said Territorial Prison at Yuma, Arizona and a sufficient Warrant for the Officers of said Territorial Prison to keep and imprison the said B.W. Birch.

Sentence   603

The United States
vs.
Mrs. Kate Nelson

The defendant being present in open Court in person and by her counsel J.F. Ross, Esq., the United States Attorney for Arizona present on the part of the United States. And this being the time heretofore fixed for passing Judgment on the defendant in this case, the Defendant Mrs. Kate Nelson was duly informed by the Court of the nature of the Indictment found against her for the crime of Adultery committed on the 19th day of November A.D., 1904 of her arraignment and plea of "Not Guilty as charged in the indictment," of the trial and the verdict of the jury on the 15th day of December A.D. 1904, Guilty as charged in the indictment. The Defendant was then asked if she had any legal cause to show why judgment should not be pronounced against her; and no sufficient cause being shown or appearing to the Court, thereupon the Court renders its judgment That, whereas, you Mrs. Kate Nelson, having been duly convicted in this court of the crime of Adultery, it is found by the Court that you are so guilty of said crime. It Is Therefore Ordered, Adjudged and Decreed and the judgment and sentence of the Court is, that you Mrs. Kate Neslon be punished by imprisonment in the Territorial Prison at Yuma, Arizona at hard labor, for a term of Two (2) years to date from Dec. 16, A.D. 1904. The defendant was then remanded to the custody of the proper Officers of said Territorial Prison, at Yuma, Arizona and It Is Further Ordered, that a certified copy of this Judgment shall be a sufficient Warrant for the said Marshal, to take, keep and safely deliver the said Mrs. Kate Nelson into the custody of the proper Officers, of said Territorial Prison, at Yuma, Arizona and a sufficient Warrant for the Officers of said Territorial Prison to keep and imprison the said Mrs. Kate Nelson.

~ Kate Nelson ~

TERRITORIAL PRISON AT YUMA, A.T.

Description of Convict

NAME:
    Kate Nelson
ALIAS:

NUMBER:
    2219
SENTENCE:
    2 yrs. from
    Dec. 16, 1904

CRIME:
    Adultery
COUNTY:
    Cochise
LEGITIMATE OCCUPATION:

NATIVITY:
    Ireland
AGE:
    38
TOBACCO:
    No

HABITS:
    Temperate
OPIUM:

RELIGION:
    Catholic
SIZE FOOT:
    5

HEIGHT:
    5' 1"
SIZE OF HEAD:

WEIGHT:
    116 lbs.
COLOR HAIR:
    Brown

COLOR EYES:
    Blue
MARRIED:
    Yes (husband living)
CAN READ:
    Yes
WHERE EDUCATED:
    Ireland

CHILDREN:
    No
CAN WRITE:
    Yes
FORMER IMPRISONMENT:

NEAREST RELATIVE:
    Mrs. George Malley (sic)
    Washington, D.C.

WHEN AND HOW DISCHARGED:
    July 1906, Expiration of sentence

PRISON RECORD

Complexion - Light   Expression - Open

⚘ Frail Prisoners in Yuma Territorial Prison ⚘

The men prisoners were continually attempting to establish contact with the women. One man was given 16 days in the dark cell for breaking into the women's quarters. Another received four days for throwing letters into the women's section. Still another was given three days for an unsuccessful attempt to climb into the women's quarters.

Pearl Eiker

Chapter 20

Pearl Eiker~No. 2616

The Bisbee Daily Review, June 11, 1907, aptly describes the case against Pearl:

"COLORED WOMAN TRIAL FOR MURDER: Tombstone, June 10--the attention of the district court was taken up today in the trial of the case of the Territory vs. Pearl Eiker, who is charged with the killing of one Lewis Clark at Douglas, on or about the 19th of April of this year. The defendant and the deceased were both colored and most of the witnesses are of the same complexion. The evidence as produced by the prosecution has been very strong and it was proven that before she went to the house where the deceased was, that she had threatened to kill him and that she had told him so herself a few hours before.

The deceased was killed with a .38 caliber revolver and shot through the heart. The killing took place in the red light district of Douglas and was caused by jealousy. From the questions asked by jurors, on the examination by the defense it is thought that they will try to prove self-defense. The following are the jurors sworn to try the case: John Bell, J.P. Peterson,

Thomas Graham, David Mitchell, I.B. Stone, Charles Monmonier, George C. Black, David Davis, C.T. Vincent, Ed Sutton, N.P. Okerstrom, and Leonard Hawkins."

Pearl's trial lasted more than two days and the jury was still dead locked. They could have agreed upon a verdict of manslaughter, but the court had not so instructed them in that event.

When going into the courtroom, the defendant heard someone call out that the jury was hung. She immediately thought that the jury had sentenced her to be hanged. Pearl became very frightened and emitted ear shattering, blood curdling screams. It took the court bailiffs some time to quiet her so that the proceedings could continue.

The jury foreman then reported to the court that they could not agree on a verdict so the judge dismissed the jury. Something about this set Eiker off again and she went into hysterical screams that continued for fifteen minutes. Finally, she was so overcome that Deputy Sheriff Ned White and Jailer Butler had to carry her from the courtroom.

Eiker's case was tried again with a new jury that found her guilty of manslaughter. Before she was sentenced, Pearl asked to make a statement. Permission was granted and she described her life and how she had become involved in her troubles. She said she would go to Yuma and serve her time, then when she was released she would live an honorable and upright life.

The district court noted that she had been found guilty of manslaughter, with recommendations for mercy, and was sentenced to three years in the Territorial Prison at Yuma.

One day Pearl Eiker complained that she was not feeling well. Doctor Ketcherside examined the prisoner, then had her moved to the prison hospital. Pearl had a bowel obstruction and there was nothing that could be done to help her.

Pearl Eiker died on January 10, 1908, and was buried in the prison cemetery.

She was the only woman to die in the Territorial Prison at Yuma.

Pearl Eiker

Tombstone Epitaph   June 16, 1907

Doings in the District Court: (In part)   Monday, June 10

The attention of the district court was taken up today in the trial of the case of the territory vs. Pearl Eikler (sic) who is charged with the killing of one Lewis Clark at Douglas on or about April 19th. The defendant and the deceased were both colored and most of the witnesses in the case are of the same complexion. The following are the jurors sworn to try the case: John Bell, Thomas Graham, I.B. Stone, George C. Black, C.T. Vencent, N.P. Okerstrom, J.P. Peterson, David Mitchel, Chas. Monmomier, David Davis, Ed Sutton, Leonard Hawkins.

The case will probably not go to the jury before tomorrow. Wednesday, June 12:

There was quite an exciting time in the district court this morning when the jury in the Pearl Eidler (sic) case was brought in, or just prior thereto. The prisoner, a colored woman, while going from the jail to the court room, overheard some one make the remark that it was "a hanged jury." She interpreted it that the jury was going to sentence her to be hanged. When she went into the court room she was trembling from head to foot and shortly after gave way to her fright and let out a series of shrieks and wails that fairly startled all court attendants. After some time she was quieted down by the court bailiffs and the jury was brought in and the foreman reported to the court that the jury was unable to agree, and were discharged by the court.

The prisoner, for some reason, again broke out and carried on for some 15 minutes and was so overcome that she had to be carried from the court room by the bailiffs.

It is said that the jury was unable to agree, standing about six to six. It is very probable that the case will be retried at the present term of court as soon as it can be reached.

The mother of the Eikler (sic) woman has been here for several weeks from her home in Texas and will remain until the case against her daughter has finally been decided.

Tombstone Epitaph   July 7, 1907

Doings in the District Court: Monday, July 1.

Territory vs. Pearl Eikner (sic), colored. Having been found guilty of manslaughter, with recommendations for mercy, was sentenced to three years at Yuma.

The defendant, when given permission to say a few words in her own behalf thanked the jury for their recommendation of mercy and, bemoaning her fate, preferred to die rather than serve a prison sentence, but concluded with the remark that perhaps the sentence would make a better woman of her.

⚘ Pearl Eiker ⚘

TERRITORIAL PRISON AT YUMA, A.T.

Description of Convict

NAME:
   Pearl Eiker (Negro)
NUMBER:
   2616
ALIAS:
SENTENCE:
   3 yrs. from July 1, 1907
CRIME:
   Manslaughter
NATIVITY:
   Texas
COUNTY:
   Cochise
AGE:
   20
LEGITIMATE OCCUPATION:
   Family Cook
TOBACCO:
   Yes
HABITS:
   Intemperate
RELIGION:
   Protestant
OPIUM:
SIZE FOOT:
   5-1/2
HEIGHT:
   5' 2-1/4"
WEIGHT:
   143 lbs.
SIZE OF HEAD:
COLOR HAIR:
   Black (Kinky)
COLOR EYES:
   Dark Maroon
CHILDREN:
MARRIED:
   Yes
CAN WRITE:
CAN READ:
   Yes
FORMER IMPRISONMENT
WHERE EDUCATED:
   Texas
NEAREST RELATIVE:
   Mother
   Mrs. Jane Eiker
   Ft. Worth, Texas
WHEN AND HOW DISCHARGED:
   Died in prison Hospital, January 10, 1908 at 4:30 a.m. of bowel obstruction.

PRISON RECORD

Forehead - medium;   Carriage - erect
Condition of Teeth - fair - right upper incisor, gold capped.
One out - right lower jaw.

Frail Prisoners in Yuma Territorial Prison

Francisca Robles

Chapter 21

Francisca Robles~No. 2645

The Arizona Republican   October 2, 1907

WIELDED A HOG KNIFE FOUND TWO VICTIMS: Marshal Moore Lands the Guilty Woman in Jail and Holds her Lover as a Witness.

Francisca Robles now lies in the county jail charged with an assault to commit murder. Ramon Moreno, her lover with whom she has been living, is being held as a witness, and Jose Garcia with a knife wound in his right lung and Ignacia Pina with a stab in the left shoulder are at the city jail under the care of the city physician, Dr. Beauchamp. It is the old story of illicit love and a bad woman's vengeful jealousy.

The beginning of this sanguinary story is in the relations existing between the four principals in the case. The two victims of the stabbing affray have been living together in one of Victor Sanchez's houses in the southeastern part of the city, while the Robles woman and her lover have been living near the old hide house. It appears that for some reason or another the Robles woman became intensely jealous of Ignacia Pina and was imbued with the idea that the latter was trying to entice her lover from her side.

Yesterday afternoon the four principals met at or near the Felimino house, in the alley between Second and Third street, this side of the M.&P. tracks, and the fire in the heart of the Robles woman flamed up as she was coming around the house, and ran onto the other pair. It was the opportunity for which she had been waiting and she was prepared with a peculiarly murderous knife having a blade seven inches long, pointed, a most ugly looking weapon.

She drew this and struck the Pina woman in the shoulder, inflicting only a slight wound, perhaps not more than an inch in depth, but which bled profusely. She then turned to Garcia before he could get away and struck a downward blow, stabbing him in the right side of the chest, the blade penetrating at least three inches. She did not carry her attack further, and Garcia started for an outbuilding near the house, but fell before he reached it. It was here that he was found by Marshal Moore and Officer Sullivan who were at once informed by one Faverno, a former dog catcher. Officer Troutman came to the scene a few minutes later and Mike Brady was summoned with his express wagon. The injured man was taken to the city jail and Dr. Beauchamp was called in to dress the wound. The woman did not appear at the time to be sufficiently injured to need attention.

The officers located the accused woman and her lover at the Porto Rico saloon, formerly called the Manila. At first she denied to Marshal Moore any knowledge of the crime whatever, knew nothing about the knife and said she had never been possessed of such described property. Ramon Moreno, however, who was standing near, immediately got busy to clean his hands of the whole affair, and told the marshal that he could show them where the knife was hid. As he directed, the bloody exhibit was found under the floor of the saloon.

Marshal Moore deputized a passerby to keep the Robles woman from escaping, and the patrol was called up and driven down to the Felimino house and the Pina woman loaded in with the lover of Robles. The patrol returned to the saloon and took in the other passenger, the cause of all the trouble, and the three were taken to the city hall. The jealous mistress was at first disposed to lay the stabbing affray on the ready witness, Moreno, but finally she admitted that she did it all and told why. She was locked up in a cell until she could be turned over to the county officials.

Dr. Beauchamp had by this time examined the wound of Garcia and pronounced it serious, but not necessarily fatal. The victim was stretched out on a cot in the basement and was suffering a great deal of pain. His wound and that of the woman were dressed and it is thought that recovery will be a matter of a few weeks, unless the condition of the wound should prove to be a septic and blood poison set in.

The Robles woman has figured in other cases and her record is said to be scarlet. She has had other lovers, but most of them are in jail or have at some time been landed there on her testimony, when she laid the offenses she probably committed herself on the shoulders of the nearest and handiest person. Her term in the pen will probably be an extended one.
FRANCISCA ROBLES CRIME: October 3, 1907

The two victims of the knife of Francisca Robles were yesterday removed to the county hospital. Neither was so badly hurt as it was thought they were the night before. The woman will be charged with assault with a deadly weapon instead of assault with intent to commit murder, for the former charge is the more easily established.

The Arizona Republican

October 4, 1907:

THE STABBER ARRAIGNED: Francisca Robles, who stabbed a man and a woman in a fit of jealousy a few days ago, was arraigned before Justice Johnstone yesterday on the charge of assault with a deadly weapon. Her preliminary hearing was set for next Monday. Both of the victims are in the county hospital. The woman is not badly hurt, but the man will not be able to be around for a day or two.

October 8, 1907:

HELD TO THE GRAND JURY: Francisca Robles who has been

❦ Frail Prisoners in Yuma Territorial Prison ❦

in jail for a week for stabbing a man and a woman living in her neighborhood in a fit of jealousy was before Justice Johnstone yesterday afternoon on the charge of committing an assault with a deadly weapon. She was held to the grand jury in the sum of $300. Her lover Ramon Moreno was also held for safe keeping.

November 2, 1907:
Criminal Docket (In part)

Francisca Robles was tried on the charge of assault with intent to commit murder. She had tried to kill her lover and a woman of whom she was jealous. She admitted on the stand that she had committed the act complained of, but justified herself on the ground that the woman had no business to steal the affections of her lover. This admission did not leave her attorney, Edward Goodwin, much ground to stand on, and he could only appeal to the jury to acquit for the reason that no amount of punishment could reform the defendant, his idea being that all punishment is, or ought to be, reformatory. He intimated, though he did not say so in so many words, that the penitentiary would not be elevated by her presence. It did not take the jury long to find her guilty. The trial order in the other case, for there were two indictments against her, was vacated.

Francisca was found guilty and sentenced to two years in the Territorial Prison, her term beginning November 2, 1907. She served 20 months of her 24 months sentence, being discharged on July 1, 1909. Probably the 4 months was good behavior time.

REGISTER of CRIMINAL ACTIONS
Maricopa County, Arizona

No. 1414   The TERRITORY OF ARIZONA
vs.
Francisca Robles

Plaintiff's Attorney - G.P. Bulland
Defendant's Attorney - E.B. Goodwin

1907
Oct
28   Filed complaint, warrant, transcript
       Assault with a Deadly Weapon - In Custody
       Exhibit "A" subp.
       Enter appear. Terr. (sic) docketed cause   28 E n t e r
       appear. deft at g J
       order waives atty   "   "   "
       order remanded
29   order or return indictment
       Filed and entered
          copy (sic)
30   Enter appear. Deft
       Order asked if her name & same
       Order arraigned & deft pleads that she is not guilty.
       Order of offense as charged.
       Order set Trial Nov. 1 order remanded
       Filed prose. 6, issued subp. of Jose Garcia & 6
       Filed defts   "   "   " Ramon Trojilla & 3
Nov.
1   Enter appear. Deft for trial
       Order trial to jury to noon recess
       Empanelling & swer. Jury, filed Jury lists
       Swerg. Interpreter & 7 wits.
       order deft. Remanded
       order trial concluded   Jury retire
       Swerg. 2 wits. order deft. Remanded
       Receiving & record and Filed verdict guilty
                              Jury discharged
       Ordered Nov. 2 at 9:30 fixed for sentence
       Ordered deft. Remanded
2   Entered appear. deft.
       Entered Judgment sentenced 2 years from to date in Terr. Prison
       Commitment   for Sheriff's return
       Filed reporter's note book (sic)
       Filed commitment on return.

TERRITORIAL PRISON AT YUMA, A.T.

Description of Convict

NAME:
    Francisca Robles
ALIAS:

CRIME :
    Assault w/deadly weapon
COUNTY:
    Maricopa
LEGITIMATE OCCUPATION:
    Prostitute
HABITS:
    Intemperate
OPIUM:
HEIGHT:
    5' 1-1/4""
SIZE OF HEAD:

COLOR EYES:
    Dark Brown
MARRIED:
    No
CAN READ:
    Poorly
WHERE EDUCATED:
    United States
WHEN AND HOW DISCHARGED:
    July 1, 1909, Expiration of sentence

NUMBER:
    2645
SENTENCE:
    2 yrs. from Nov. 2, 1907
NATIVITY:
    Mexico
AGE:
    37
TOBACCO:
    Yes
RELIGION:
    Catholic
SIZE FOOT:
WEIGHT:
    125 lbs.
COLOR HAIR:
    Black
CHILDREN:
    None
CAN WRITE:
    Poorly
FORMER IMPRISONMENT:

NEAREST RELATIVE:
    Has Parents (don't know)

PRISON RECORD

Scars: One scar right cheek, one mole - size of a pea behind lobe of right ear

Chapter 22
Saferina Garcia~No. 2757

Arizona Bulletin November 29, 1907

There was shooting disturbance in the east part of town early Wednesday morning. A Mexican woman named Saferina Garcia went to the house of a woman named Gonzales and demanded admittance. Being refused she fired a couple of shots through a window and one through a door. The Gonzales woman and three children were sleeping in the room and the bullets passed just over the bed. The shots were heard by the officers who went to the locality and gathered the aggregation into the county jail. The neighborhood is sometimes referred to as Little Chihuahua and is one of the toughest in town, both Americans and Mexicans of low character hanging out there. The Garcia woman was fined $60 in Justice Austen's court and committed to jail in default of payment.

February 15, 1908
Judge Austen gave Saferina Garcia a sixty-day sentence this week, for raising a rough-house.

May 1, 1908 **The Graham Guardian**
Saferina Garcia, who attempted to liberate some of the prisoners in the county jail several weeks ago, was sentenced to one year in the Yuma prison.

❧ Frail Prisoners in Yuma Territorial Prison ❧

TERRITORIAL PRISON AT YUMA, A.T.

Description of Convict

NAME:
    Miss Saferina Garcia

ALIAS:

CRIME :
    Felony

COUNTY:
    Graham

LEGITIMATE OCCUPATION:
    House Maid

HABITS:
    Intemperate

OPIUM:
    No

HEIGHT:
    4' 7-1/4"

SIZE OF HEAD:

COLOR EYES:
    Brown

MARRIED:
    No

CAN READ:
    No

WHERE EDUCATED:

NUMBER:
    2757
    Com. #1226 - 5 Jud. Dist.

SENTENCE:
    One year, one day from
    May 1, 1908

NATIVITY:
    Mexico

AGE:
    25

TOBACCO:
    Yes

RELIGION:
    Catholic

SIZE FOOT:
    3-1/2

WEIGHT:
    117 lbs.

COLOR HAIR:
    Black

CHILDREN:

CAN WRITE:
    No

FORMER IMPRISONMENT:

NEAREST RELATIVE:
    Parents - No - Sister
    Margarita Garcia,
    Douglas, Az.

WHEN AND HOW DISCHARGED:
    March 1, 1909, Expiration of sentence
    Graham Guardian 1-8-08

PRISON RECORD

*Attempted to liberate some prisoners from Co. jail.
More description: Complexion - dark; Forehead - medium low;
Physical pecul. - short, heavy built.

Chapter 23

Ada Parks~No. 2833

Ada Parks was brought before Elmer Longui, Justice of the Peace on June 30, 1908 and charged with a felony. She was admitted to bail in the sum of $200, which was supplied by B.F. Sweetwood and Jesus Quijada.

On September 21, 1908, Parks was accused by the Grand Jury of Coconino County of the crime of Grand Larceny committed as follows: Ada Parks on or about June 28, 1908, did steal and carry away from one John Mure, three ten dollar bills, one one dollar bill, one dime, and one penny, all lawful money of the United States and of the aggregate value of $31.11; and one pair of cuff buttons being the personal property of John Mure.

When brought into court for her hearing on September 22, 1908, Ada Parks entered a plea of not guilty. The court then set her trial date as September 23, 1908.

John Mure, Herbert Woods, and Lieutenant W.A. Olds took the oath and testified for the Territory. The prosecution then closed its testimony.

Jesus Quijado, Felipe Chaves, Jesse Franklin, and a Mrs.

⚹ Frail Prisoners in Yuma Territorial Prison ⚹

Ebert took oath and testified in the behalf of the defendant. Ada Parks then took the stance and testified after which the defense closed its testimony.

W.G. Dickinson, Jury Foreman, announced the jury's verdict, "We, the jury, find the defendant guilty as charged and recommend the mercy of the Court in her behalf."

The Arizona Republican, September 27, 1908, noted part of the court week at Flagstaff:

"Wednesday morning the trial cases were begun, the first one taken up being the case of Ada Parks, a negress, from Williams, who was charged with robbing a certain negro of the same town of money and other valuables. The case was given to the jury at noon, but it was 8:30 that night before it had reached a verdict. The verdict was guilty."

On September 25, 1908, the judge sentenced Ada Parks: By the verdict of twelve good and lawful men you were found guilty of the crime of Grand Larceny on the 23rd day of September, A.D. 1908. You are to be punished as follows: That you, Ada Parks, be confined and imprisoned in the Territorial Prison in the Territory of Arizona for a period of one year, and that your term of imprisonment shall begin on the 25th day of September A.D. 1908.

Ada Parks served 10 months of her 12 months sentence, being discharged July 29, 1909.

Ada Parks

Indictment by the Grand Jury

IN THE DISTRICT COURT OF THE FOURTH JUDICIAL DISTRICT
Of the Territory of Arizona,
in and for the County of Coconino

INDICTMENT
The Territory of Arizona, Plaintiff,
vs.
Ada Parks, Defendant
September Term, A.D. 1908

Ada Parks is accused by the Grand Jury of the County of Coconino, Territory of Arizona, by this Indictment, found on the 21st, day of September A.D. 1908, of the crime of Grand Larceny committed as follows, to-wit: The said Ada Parks on or about the 28th day of June, A.D. 1908, and before the finding of this Indictment at the County of Coconino, Territory of Arizona, then and there being, did willfully, unlawfully and feloniously steal, take and carry away from the person of one John Mure, then and there being, three Ten Dollar bills, one certain One Dollar bill, one certain Dime and one certain Penny, all lawful money of the United States of America and of the aggregate value of Thirty-one Dollars and eleven cents ($31.11) and one pair of cuff buttons, said lawful money of the United States of America and said one pair of cuff buttons, said lawful money of the United States of America and said one pair of cuff buttons being then and there the personal property of him, the said John Mure.

contrary to the from, force and effect of the Statute in such cases made and provided and against the peace and dignity of the Territory of Arizona.

Henry F. Ashurst
District Attorney.

Charles Babbitt, Foreman of Grand Jury
N.G. Layton, Clerk
John Mure and Herbert Woods, Witnesses examined before the Grand Jury.

Summary of Court Proceedings

September 22, 1908

Territory of Arizona)
vs.
Ada Parks
No. 336

This being the time set for hearing the plea of Ada Parks, the defendant herein, she was brought into Court for that purpose, and being in Court she was asked for her plea, whereupon she replied, "I'm not Guilty." The Court fixed the date of her trial for Wednesday morning, September 23rd at 9:30 o'clock.

September 23, 1908

This cause coming on regularly for hearing, this 23rd day September, 1908. Twenty-four jurors were called, and sworn as to their qualifications as jurors, in this cause and from the list of the jurors passed by the respective attorneys, and the defendant being in Court with her Attorney, X.N. Steeves, and the District Attorney appearing for the Territory, the following named jurors were sworn to try the cause: G.T. Herrington, Al Sanford, W.G. Dickinson, Al Hawkins, J.S. Roth, Thos. Frier, Burton A. Doyle, D.B. Lovell, W.H. Carroll, Clement Mayer, J.H. Bird, A.S. Alvord who took their seats in the box, and the cause proceeded to trial.

John Mure, Lieut. W.A. Olds, and Herbert Woods were sworn and testified for the Territory after which the plaintiff announced its testimony closed.

Jesus Quijado, Mrs. Ebert, Felipe Chaves and Jesse Franklin were sworn and testified for the defense.

Ada Parks, the defendant herein, was sworn and testified in her own behalf, after which the defense announced its testimony closed.

Henry F. Ashurst, District Attorney, addressed the jury in behalf of the Territory and was followed by Mr. X.N. Steeves for the defense which closed the argument.

The Court instructed the jury as to the law and the evidence and the nature of the several kinds of verdict. E.S. Carlos was sworn as bailiff, and the jury retired for deliberation in his charge.

Summary of Court Proceedings

Court ordered recess until 1:30 o'clock p.m. this day.

The jury in this cause was returned into Court by the bailiff and the defendant being present by her Attorney, X.N. Steeves. Upon roll call by the Clerk, all jurors answered to their names. Being asked if they agreed upon a verdict, they answered, "we have." Being directed to announce the verdict, they announced through Foreman, the following verdict:

"We, the jury, find the defendant guilty as charged and recommend the mercy of the Court in her behalf.

Signed W.G. Dickinson, Foreman

The jury being asked this was their verdict as found, they each answered, "it is."

The verdict was recorded in open court in the presence of the jury, and the Court discharged the jury until Thursday morning, September 24, 1908 at 9:30 o'clock.

The Court ordered an adjournment until Thursday September 24th, 1908 at 9:30 o'clock.

Richard Sloan, (sic)
Judge.

~ Frail Prisoners in Yuma Territorial Prison ~

SENTENCE ~ ADA PARKS

IN THE DISTRICT COURT OF THE
FOURTH JUDICIAL DISTRICT,
Of the Territory of Arizona, in and for the County of Coconino

Territory of Arizona
            vs.   No. 336
Ada Parks

    In this cause this day, to-wit: The 25th day of September A.D. 1908, having been fixed by the court for passing sentence on the defendant Ada Parks she was brought into court, and her counsel, N. Stevens, Esq. And Henry Ashurst District Attorney, being present, and defendant standing in court, the following judgement and sentence was pronounced by the court and ordered entered.

    You, Ada Parks, having been indicted by the Grand Jury, of the County of Coconino at the September term, 1908, of this court, of the crime of Grand Larceny, to which indictment upon your arraignment you plead not guilty and put yourself upon the country, to wit: By the verdict of twelve good and lawful men you were found guilty of the crime of Grand Larceny on the 23rd day of September, A.D. 1908.

    Have you now anything to offer as legal cause why judgment and sentence should not be pronounced against you?

    No legal cause being by you shown, the judgment of the court is that you Ada Parks are guilty of the crime of Grand Larceny and judgment and sentence thereon is, that you be punished therefor as follows, to-wit:

    That you Ada Parks be confined and imprisoned in the Territorial prison in the Territory of Arizona for a period of one year, and that your term of imprisonment shall begin on the 25th day of September A.D., 1908.

Territory of Arizona)
County of Coconino) SS

    I, N.G. Layton Clerk of the District Court, of the Fourth Judicial District of the Territory of Arizona in and for the County of Coconino, do hereby certify the foregoing to be a true copy of an original judgment, sentence and order of said court as appears on the minute record and is now on file in my office.

    In testimony whereof, I have hereunto set my hand and affixed the seal of said court on the 25th day of September A.D. 1908.

                                                                  N.G. Layton, Clerk

~ Ada Parks ~

TERRITORIAL PRISON AT YUMA, A.T.

Description of Convict

NAME:
  Ada Parks (Negro Female)
ALIAS:

CRIME:
  Grand Larceny
COUNTY:
  Coconino
LEGITIMATE OCCUPATION:
  House maid
HABITS:
  Temperate
OPIUM:
  No
HEIGHT:
  5' 4-1/4"
SIZE OF HEAD:

COLOR EYES:
  Black
MARRIED:
  No
CAN READ:
  No
WHERE EDUCATED:
WHEN AND HOW DISCHARGED:
  July 29, 1909, Expiration of sentence

NUMBER:
  2833
SENTENCE:
  One year from
  Sept. 25, 1908
NATIVITY:
  Alabama
AGE:
  22
TOBACCO:
  No
RELIGION:
  Methodist
SIZE FOOT:
  6
WEIGHT:
  127 lbs.
COLOR HAIR:
  Black (Kinky)
CHILDREN:
  2
CAN WRITE:
  No
FORMER IMPRISONMENT:

NEAREST RELATIVE:

PRISON RECORD

Az. Republican - 9-27-1908
More description:
Forehead - medium
Expression - good
Complexion - dark maroon

❧ Frail Prisoners in Yuma Territorial Prison ❧

Pinkie Dean

Chapter 24

Pinkie Dean~No. 2842

On April 22, 1908, a drunken negro woman slashed Billy Hennessy, a well-known miner at Kofa. At first it was believed to have been a fatal slashing as there were six ugly, fearsome wounds--one of them exposing much of the man's intestines. This negress is known as Pinkie Dean and the knifing occurred in her apartment in the rear of a saloon.

She was held without bail for the Grand Jury by Justice Taylor. Constable Bob Bechtel took her to Yuma and placed her in the county jail. In the beginning she claimed that she was drunk and had no knowledge of her crime. Others seemed to indicate that the slashing was premeditated.

Dean was transferred to the Pima County jail on a writ of habeas corpus as the Yuma County jail was unfit and unsafe. This lodging was to be at the expense of Yuma County. She was delivered to the Pima County Sheriff May 21, 1908.

Pinkie was indicted by the Grand Jury for the assault upon the miner at Kofa, (the miner recovered), with a deadly weapon. During her trial on October 14, 1908, the jury was instructed in this manner:

"If the jury believes from the evidence that the prosecuting witness, Hennessy, entered the tent, house, or dwelling place of the defendant, Pinkie Dean, and there first assaulted the defendant without any reasonable or justifiable cause, and that the defendant was in great fear of her life or of great bodily harm from the prosecuting witness Hennessy, and that from the surrounding circumstances she had reasonable grounds for such fear and acting under such fear, struck the witness, they should acquit the defendant."

Apparently, the jury did not believe that Pinkie Dean feared anything or was defending herself. They pronounced her guilty as charged. The court sentenced her to two years and six months in the Territorial Prison beginning on October 10, 1908.

Pinkie served two years of her sentence. During her imprisonment Florence Penitentiary was finished and she was transferred there. She was released on October 9, 1910.

❧ Frail Prisoners in Yuma Territorial Prison ☙

Arizona Sentinel   April 29, 1908

KOFA FURNISHES BLOODY TRAGEDY
A Negress Stabs Billy Hennessy, Probably Fatally

At Kofa last Thursday afternoon Billy Hennessy, a well-known miner, was fearfully slashed with a knife in the hands of a drunken negro woman, and it was thought he could not recover. There were six ugly knife wounds, one exposing the intestines. The slasher is a negress known as "Pinkie Dean," and the row occurred in her apartment in the rear of a saloon.

She was held to the grand jury without bail by Justice Taylor and was brought to Yuma by Constable Bob Bechtel and placed in the county jail. The woman claims to have no knowledge of the crime, and that she was drunk. Circumstances, however, seem to indicate that her act was premeditated.

May 20, 1908

Bill Hennessy, the miner who was so brutally slashed with a knife by a negress at Kofa some days ago, was brought to Yuma last Thursday by Constable Robert Bechtel and placed in the hospital.

October 7, 1908

District Court (in part): Indicted by the Grand Jury - "Pinkie" Dean, a colored woman, for assault upon a miner at Kofa some months ago.

October 14, 1908

District Court (in part): "Pinkie Dean" was convicted of murderous assault upon a miner at Kofa and sentenced to two years and a half on the hill.

~ Pinkie Dean ~

TERRITORIAL PRISON AT YUMA, A.T.

Description of Convict

NAME:
    Pinkie Dean (Female Negro)

ALIAS:

CRIME:
    Assault w/deadly weapon

COUNTY:
    Yuma

LEGITIMATE OCCUPATION:
    Prostitute

HABITS:
    Intemperate

OPIUM:
    Yes

HEIGHT:

SIZE OF HEAD:

COLOR EYES:
    Dark Maroon

MARRIED:
    No

CAN READ:
    Yes

WHERE EDUCATED:
    Kansas (Public)

NUMBER:
    2842

SENTENCE:
    2 yrs. 6 mos. from Oct. 10, 1908

NATIVITY:
    Texas

AGE:
    20

TOBACCO:
    Yes

RELIGION:
    Baptist

SIZE FOOT:

WEIGHT:

COLOR HAIR:
    Black (Kinky)

CHILDREN:

CAN WRITE:
    Yes

FORMER IMPRISONMENT:

NEAREST RELATIVE:
    Sister: Mrs. Celia Williams, Shawnee, Okla

WHEN AND HOW DISCHARGED:
    Transferred to Florence. Discharged by expiration of sentence October 9, 1910.

PRISON RECORD

March 7, 1909   5 days in solitary for fighting and quarreling.
Arizona Sentinel: 4-29-08, 5-20-08, 9-20-08, 10-14-08
More description: Carriage - erect, Forehead - Low
One right upper front tooth out.

Frail Prisoners in Yuma Territorial Prison

Angelita Berdusco

Chapter 25

Angelita Berdusco

Angelita was accused of the crime of adultery by having carnal knowledge of the body of one Alonzo Martini, a male person, who was not the husband of Angelito Berdusco; the said Angelita Berdusco being married and having a husband in full life contrary to the form of Act of Congress of March 3, 1887 -(2x United States Statutes at Large 635); in such cases provided, and against the peace of the United States of America and their dignity.

At her arraignment Angelita entered a plea of not guilty of the offense charged in the indictment. The date was October 21, 1908. The next day she changed her plea to guilty as charged.

The court rendered its judgment, the judge saying: "Angelita Berdusco, having been duly convicted in this Court of the crime of adultery, it is found that you are so guilty of said crime on your own plea. The judgment and sentence of the Court is, that you, Angelita Berdusco, be punished in Territorial Prison of the Territory of Arizona, for a term of ten months, to date from August 25, 1908."

Angelita served 9 months of her 12 months sentence and was released on May 17, 1909.

Court Record - Angelita Berdusco #2871

COMPLAINT

UNITED STATES of AMERICA
vs.
Angelita Berdusco

No. 727

UNITED STATES OF AMERICA) ss.
Third Judicial District of Arizona)

    Before me C.W. Johnstone, a United States Commissioner for the Third Judicial District of Arizona, duly appointed to administer oaths, to take acknowledgments of bail, and also to take depositions of witnesses in civil causes pending in the Courts of the United States, pursuant to the provisions of the Act of Congress in that behalf, personally came George A. (Sic) Christy, Asst U.S. Atty for Arizona being duly sworn, according to law, deposes and says upon information and belief that, heretofore, to-wit: On or about the 20th day of August A.D. 1908, one Angelita Berdusco at the County of Maricopa in the Third Judicial District of Arizona Territory, did commit the crime of adultery by having carnal knowledge of the body of one Alonzo Martini, a male person, the said Alonzo Martini being then and there not the husband of said Angelita Berdusco, and she the said Angelita Berdusco being then and there married and having a husband in full life contrary to the form of Act of Congress of Mch. 3rd 1887 - (2x United States Statutes at Large 635), in such cases provided, and against the peace of the United States of America and their dignity.

    Wherefore, affiant prays that said Angelita Berdusco may be apprehended by whatever name she may be known, and dealt with according to law.

George A. Christy

Subscribed and sworn to before me, this 21st day of August 1908.
C.W. Johnstone
U.S. Commissioner

I certify that the foregoing is a true copy of the complaint on file in my office.
U.S. Commissioner

Filed August 21st, 1908   C.W. Johnstone, U.S. Commissioner
Filed Sept. 2, 1908   Elias P. Dunlevy, Clerk District Court
By J.S. Jenckes, Jr. Depty.

Angelita Berdusco

Court Records — Angelita Berdusco

UNITED STATES OF AMERICA
IN THE DISTRICT COURT OF THE THIRD JUDICIAL DISTRICT OF THE TERRITORY OF ARIZONA

(Having and exercising the same jurisdiction under the Constitution and Laws of the United States as is vested in the Circuit and District Courts of the United States.)

UNITED STATES OF AMERICA) Plaintiff) vs. Angelita Berdusco, Defendant	October Term, A.D. 1908 October 22nd, 1908 Present, Hon. Edward Kent, District Judge Convicted of Adultery.

The defendant being present in open Court in person and by E.B. Goodwin Esq., her attorney, J.L.B. Alexander, Esq., the United States Attorney for Arizona, being present on the part of the United States. And this being the time heretofore fixed for passing judgment on the defendant in this case, the defendant, Angelita Berdusco, was duly informed by the Court of the nature of the indictment found against her for the crime of adultery committed on or about the 20th day of August, A.D. 1908; of her arraignment and plea of "Not Guilty of the offense charged in the indictment," on the 21st day of October, A.D. 1908, and of her subsequent plea on October 22nd, A.D. 1908, that she was guilty.

The defendant was then asked if she had any legal cause to show why judgment should not be pronounced against her, and no sufficient cause being shown or appearing to the Court, thereupon the Court renders its judgment; That, whereas you, Angelita Berdusco, having been duly convicted in this Court of the crime of adultery, it is found by the Court that you are so guilty of said crime on your own plea.

IT IS THEREFORE ORDERED, ADJUDGED AND DECREED, and the judgment and sentence of the Court is, that you, Angelita Berdusco, be punished in the Territorial Prison of the Territory of Arizona, for a term of ten (10) months, to date from August 25th, A.D. 1908.

The defendant was then remanded to the custody of the United States Marshal for said Arizona Territory, to be by him delivered into the custody of the proper officers of the Territorial Prison.

AND IT IS FURTHER ORDERED, that a certified copy of this judgment shall be sufficient warrant for the said Marshal to take, keep and safely deliver the said Angelita Berdusco into custody of the proper officers of said Territorial Prison, and a sufficient warrant for the officers of said Territorial Prison to keep and imprison the said Angelita Berdusco.

Chief Justice and Judge of
Third Judicial District

❧ Frail Prisoners in Yuma Territorial Prison ❦

UNITED STATES OF AMERICA)
Territory of Arizona) ss.
Third Judicial District)

I, ELIAS P. DUNLEVY, Clerk of the District Court for the Third Judicial District of Arizona, do hereby certify the above and foregoing to be a true and correct copy of the order of judgment made and entered of record in said Court in the above entitled action on the 22nd day of October A.D. 1908, as the same now remains of record in my office.

WITNESS my hand and the seal of said Court this 23rd day of October, A.D. 1908.

_____
　　　　　　　　　　　　　　　　Clerk

The Arizona Republican　　　　　　　　　　　August 17, 1908

"MISS PANOCHE" ELOPES
THIS TIME IT'S A GO:　She Takes Her Sister and
　　　　　　　　　　　Martini the Showman With Her

"Miss Panoche" has finally eloped in earnest, and she took her sister with her. "Miss Panoche" a funny nickname for Miss Adela Padilla, came into prominence last week in connection with an escapade involving another young woman and Martini, who has been giving sleight of hand and juggling exhibitions at the Airdome. Either "Miss Panoche" or the other girl hired a horse and buggy, which was afterward heard of at Glendale, and it was learned that Martini had accompanied the women to that point.

~ Angelita Berdusco ~

The story came out the next day, and "Miss Panoche" was around with an indignant explanation which did not throw a great deal of light on the subject. The burden of it was that she did not have anything to do with the affair. But yesterday morning she and her sister, Miss Angelia Padilla, left for the north on the 2 o'clock train accompanied by Martini and his assistant, Irenjo.

The girls were missed by their parents yesterday morning and inquiry brought out the direction they had taken. It was also learned that the showmen had accompanied them.

Their father appeared before Justice Johnstone and asked for a warrant for the arrest of the two men. "Miss Panoche" is under the age of which men can elope with her without committing a crime. The sister is older and has been married, though she is known by her maiden name.

Telegrams were sent to all stations along the S.F., P.&P., inquiring about the quartette, but last night no information had been received.

THE CHILD STEALERS ARE AT WICHENBURG: Drove Across the Country to Meet Two Girls But Will Have to Face a Serious Charge

Joseph Irenjo and Carlos Martini, two vaudeville performers, who have been wanted to a case of child stealing were apprehended in Wickenburg last evening and Constable Murphy who has been working on the case ever since the disappearance of Adela Padilla and Angelita Padilla Sunday, left this morning on the two o'clock train to bring the two men to Phoenix.

It is a very serious charge which the vaudeville artists will face, in fact they can be put through on two or three counts. The men have been very intimate with these girls while in this city despite the efforts of the mother to prevent their being together.

Sunday morning they disappeared rather quietly and mysteriously and all sorts of tales were afloat and the mother was much exercised. Constable Murphy investigated and learned from the conductor that the girls and the jugglers had left

Phoenix on the two o'clock train and that the girls went to Wickenburg. Constable Murphy then informed the Wickenburg authorities to be on the lookout for he believed that it was the intention of the men to meet them there. Constable Murphy ascertained that Irenjo and Martini had assisted them in getting away, bought the tickets and accompanied them as far as Glendale.

Later he found out that the two men had kept out of sight as much as possible and taking two single rigs had embarked at Glendale for a cross country drive. This further confirmed him in the opinion that the lovers would meet the girls at the Hassayampa town and he again communicated with the Wickenburg officer. Yesterday evening the jugglers drove into town and the officer spotted them and when Constable Murphy arrives this morning they will be arrested. The younger Padilla girl is only sixteen while the older one is about twenty-one.

August 21: VAUDEVILLE ARTISTS ARE NOW IN LIMBO: Will Be Arraigned today on the Charge of Child Stealing

Joseph Irenjo and Carlos Martini, charged with child stealing, in the case of Adela and Angelita Padilla, were brought back to Phoenix yesterday by Constable Murphy and will be arraigned today before Justice Johnstone. The case is said to be very strong against the vaudeville performers but the outcome of the case is uncertain. They can be held on different counts. One of the girls is a grass widow while the other is said to be only 16 years old.

Constable Murphy found the men and arrested them before daybreak at Wickenburg. One couple was in a lodging house up town, the other at a house near the river. When Murphy went in through the window after them, they were found asleep and in a state of dishabille.

They made no protest and took their arrest rather indifferently. Both the girls and their juggler-lovers were brought here, though the former were not placed under arrest.

☞ Angelita Berdusco ☜

The Arizona Republican   August 17, 20, 21 & 22, 1908

THE JUGGLERS ARRAIGNED: L. Martini and Yreneo Romero, the two vaudeville artists who had been going under different names, will be arraigned today before Justice Johnstone charged with child stealing. A new charge has been entered against Romero, that of rape. Also a complaint has been filed before Justice Johnstone as United States commissioner, against Martini and Angelita Padilla Berdusco, charging them with adultery.

August 26, 1908   HELD TO THE GRAND JURY:

Mrs. Angelita Berdusco and Martini, the juggler, were arraigned before Justice Johnstone yesterday. The former was held to answer to the grand jury for a statutory offense under a bond of $300, while Martini was held on the same charge under a bond of $500. They were placed in jail and so far no bail has been given, though efforts are being made to secure it.

August 23, 1908:   THEY WERE MARRIED: The case of child stealing against Romero, the juggler, was settled yesterday in Justice Johnstone's court by the marriage of the accused prisoner and Adella Padilla. Angelita Berdusco and Martini were formally charged with adultery and their hearing will be had Monday afternoon at 4 o'clock.

October 23, 1908   DOOM PRONOUNCED ON PRISONERS: (In part)

Alonzo Martini, the magician, and Angelita Berdusco, who had eloped and were captured at Wickenburg, pleaded guilty to a violation of the Edmunds Act and were each sentenced to ten months in the county jail (sic).

Daily Arizona Silver Belt June 6, 1909

Higinio Berdusco, who at the last term of the Phoenix district court, sent his wife to the penitentiary for violation of the Edmunds Act, is now on trial for a similar charge and will probably follow his spouse to the territorial prison.

⚜ Frail Prisoners in Yuma Territorial Prison ⚜

TERRITORIAL PRISON AT YUMA, A.T.

Description of Convict

NAME:
    Angelita Berdusco
ALIAS:

CRIME:
    Adultery
COUNTY:
    Maricopa
LEGITIMATE OCCUPATION:
    Housemaid, Laundry worker
HABITS:
    Temperate
OPIUM:
    No
HEIGHT:
    5' 2-1/2"
SIZE OF HEAD:

COLOR EYES:
    Nearly Black
MARRIED:
    Yes
CAN READ:
    Yes
WHERE EDUCATED:
    Phoenix, Az.

NUMBER:
    2871
SENTENCE:
    10 mos. from
    August 25, 1908
NATIVITY:
    Phoenix, Arizona
AGE:
    23
TOBACCO:
    Yes
RELIGION:
    Catholic
SIZE FOOT:
    4
WEIGHT:
    127 lbs.
COLOR HAIR:
    Black
CHILDREN:
    No
CAN WRITE:
    Yes
FORMER IMPRISONMENT:

NEAREST RELATIVE:
    Mother - Cruz Macias (sic)
    Phoenix

WHEN AND HOW DISCHARGED:
    May 17, 1909, Expiration of sentence.
    Arizona Republican 8/17-26-08

PRISON RECORD

More description:
Forehead - Broad
Teeth - sound, full set

☙ Eulogia Bracamonte ❧

Chapter 26

Eulogia Bracamonte~No. 2905

The Arizona Republican   February 25, 1907

A FAMILY ARRESTED: Officer Olean returned yesterday morning from Florence with Refugio Bracamonte and his wife, Eulogia, who were wanted here on the complaint of a former neighbor, Jesus S. Hartigan, charging them with petty larceny in the theft of various articles from his place in the southern part of the city. The warrant for their arrest was sworn out before Justice Kyle on Saturday. They will be given a hearing this morning. In the meantime they are guests of the sheriff.

The Arizona Republican   July 20, 1908

AN AFFECTIONATE WIFE: Refugio Bracamonte, some months ago, fell a victim to smiles and caprices of one Eulogia, who was at the time a society leader in the tenderloin, and married her. Saturday night he fell before her again but this time

177

her weapons were a pen knife and a good right arm, with which she wielded it. She also availed herself of the advantages of a flank movement by which she was able to approach from the rear and sliver his hide to shoe strings before she was diverted from her pleasing occupation. Just how many rawhide thongs Refugio's back will yield in a season was not learned but his wounds are not deep and he is not dangerously hurt. It is reported that Eulogia said yesterday that she hoped she had succeeded in making herself a widow, not of the grass variety, but real weeds.

July 21, 1908:

THE HUSBAND SLASHER:

Eulogia Bracamonte, who tried to make ribbons out of her husband, Refugio Bracamonte, was arraigned before Justice Johnstone yesterday and her hearing was set for this morning. It is understood that the woman had a great deal of provocation and it is the consensus of opinion by those who know the Bracamontes that any change that the woman could have made in her husband, would necessarily have been for the better.

July 22, 1908:

SHE'S SAFE FOR A WHILE:

Refugio Bracamonte of whom his wife tried to make shoe strings last Sunday night need be under no apprehension of danger from that quarter at least before the meeting of the next grand jury. The woman had a preliminary trial before Justice Johnstone yesterday and was held to the grand jury in the sum of $200. That is not very much on the face of it, but it will probably hold Mrs. Eulogia as tight as if it were $2000.

Eulogia Bracamonte

Nov. 6, 1908

Preliminary Hearing of the Grand Jury:

Eulogia Bracamonte for sticking a knife in the back of her husband. The husband is now in jail awaiting the action of the grand jury on the charge of robbery. Note: Charges were dropped against him.

The Arizona Republican   **Nov. 17, 1908**

DISTRICT COURT:

The trial of criminal cases was resumed in the district court yesterday morning. When the case of Eulogia Bracamonte, indicted for an assault upon her husband with a deadly weapon was called, she withdrew her plea of not guilty, entered one of guilty and will be sentenced this morning.

November 18, 1908

SENTENCED TO YUMA:

Eulogia Bracamonte, who pleaded guilty in district court day before yesterday to a murderous assault upon her husband, was yesterday sentenced by Judge Kent to one year in the territorial prison, the sentence to date from the time of her arrest.

Eulogia served 11 months of her 12 months sentence with one month off for good behavior.

~ **Frail Prisoners in Yuma Territorial Prison** ~

REGISTER of CRIMINAL ACTIONS
Maricopa County, Arizona

No. 1318
THE TERRITORY OF ARIZONA
vs
Eulogia Bracamonte
1908

G.P. Bullard Goodwin
Plaintiff's Attorney

E.B.
Defendant's Attorney

Assault with a deadly weapon.

Sept.	2	Filed Complt., warrant, subp. Transcript. Ent. appear. Territory Docketed cause
Nov.	4	Ent. appear. Deft. impanelling grand jury In custody Ordered appear. of deft in person with Ordered deft. remanded after impanelling J.P.
	5	Order on return of indictment Filed and entered Certified Copy
	6	Entered appear deft for arraignment Order asked true name & same pleads that she is not guilty of the offense chged.
	6	Order set trial Nov. 16, order remanded
	10	Enter. issued on of Ramon Flores
	16	Enter. on upon return Enter. appear. deft for trial Enter. deft. withdraws plea not guilty. Enter. plea that she is guilty offense chgd. Nov. 17 at 9:30 fixed for sentence Remanded
	17	Enter appear. of deft for sentence Judgment is imprisoned 1 year from July 9, 1908 in Territorial Prison Enter Commitment
	30	Filed Supt. receipt for prisoner.

⚜ Eulogia Bracamonte ⚜

TERRITORIAL PRISON AT YUMA, A.T.

Description of Convict

NAME:
    Eulogia Bracamonte
ALIAS:

CRIME:
    Assault w/deadly weapon
COUNTY:
    Maricopa
LEGITIMATE OCCUPATION:

HABITS:
    Temperate
OPIUM:
    No
HEIGHT:
    4' 11-1/2"
SIZE OF HEAD:

COLOR EYES:
    Brown
MARRIED:
    Yes
CAN READ:
    No
WHERE EDUCATED:

NUMBER:
    2905
SENTENCE:
    Com. #1318 3rd Jud. Dist.
    1 yr. From July 19, 1908
NATIVITY:
    Florence A.T.
AGE:
    35
TOBACCO:
    Yes
RELIGION:
    Catholic
SIZE FOOT:
    4-1/2
WEIGHT:
    111 lbs.
COLOR HAIR:
    Black
CHILDREN:
    Four
CAN WRITE:
    No
FORMER IMPRISONMENT:

NEAREST RELATIVE:
    Husband - Refugio Bracamonte, Phoenix
    Mother - Carmen A. Lopez, Phoenix

WHEN AND HOW DISCHARGED:
    June 7, 1909, Expiration of sentence.

PRISON RECORD

Forehead - Medium - low   Carriage - Stooping
Condition of teeth - Good, One Right lower tooth out.

Frail Prisoners in Yuma Territorial Prison

Angelita Sonoqui

Chapter 27

Angelita Sonoqui~No. 2942

Jose Montoya and Angelita Sonoqui had been served warrants that they had violated the Edmonds Act (adultery).

The complaint was made on November 2, 1908, by Jesus Sonoqui, who swore that Jose Montoya and Angelita Sonoqui, did have carnal knowledge of the body of each other, she, being a married woman and having a husband in full life and he, Jose Montoya, not being her husband.

On December 19, 1908, they were arraigned on an indictment charging that they had committed adultery. Both defendants pled former jeopardy and not guilty. Bail was fixed at $250 each and the trial was set for March 1, 1909.

Their attorney, E.B. Goodwin, made the plea for former jeopardy, saying that the defendants had been tried for adultery within the last three years. Such a plea generated a great deal of amusement, but Goodwin insisted that the evidence presented against the defendants was remarkably similar to that used against them at the first trial.

The trial took place on March 2, 1909. M.A. Ivy, George Kirkland, Antilano Roblez, Maria Roblez, Maria Morales, Joe Porterie, and Novatus Benzing were sworn and testified in behalf of the government.

Montoya Sonoqui and C.W. Johnstone were sworn and testified for the defendants. After the closing arguments from both sides had been heard the jury retired. When they returned the jury foreman, J.L. Irwin, gave their verdict:

"We, the Jury, duly impanelled and sworn in the above entitled action, upon our oaths, do find the defendants guilty."

Montoya and Sonoqui were sentenced on March 4, 1909, the former to eight months and the latter to four months in the Territorial Prison. Angelita served her prison term of four months and was discharged on July 3, 1909.

Court Records - Angelita Sonoqui #2942

COMPLAINT:

UNITED STATES of AMERICA
VS.
Jose M. Montoya and Angelita Sonoqui

UNITED STATES of AMERICA)
                                                    ss. No. 734
3rd Judicial District of Arizona)

    Before me, C.W. Johnstone, a United States Commissioner for the Third Judicial District of Arizona, duly appointed to administer oaths, to take acknowledgments of bail, and also to take depositions of witnesses in civil causes pending in the Courts of the United States, pursuant to the provisions of the Act of Congress in that behalf, personally came Jesus Sonoqui who being duly sworn, according to law deposes and says that, heretofore, to-wit: he the said Jose M. Montoya and she the said Angelita Sonoqui, did then and there have carnal knowledge of the body of each other she, the said Angelita Sonoqui then and there being a married woman and having a husband in full life and he the said Jose M. Montoya then and there not being the husband of the said Angelita Sonoqui contrary to the form of Section No._____ Revised Statutes of the United States of America, in such cases provided, and against the peace of the United States of America and their dignity.

    Wherefore, affiant prays that said Jose M. Montoya and Angelita Sonoqui may be apprehended by whatever name they may be known, and dealt with according to law.

                                      Jesus Sonoqui

Subscribed and sworn to before me, this 2nd day of November 1908.

                                      C.W. Johnstone
                                      U.S. Commissioner

I certify that the foregoing is a true copy of the complaint on file in my office.
                                        U.S. Commissioner

        Filed Nov. 2, 1908   C.W. Johnstone, U.S. Commissioner
        Filed Nov. 16, 1908   Elias F. Dunlevy, Clerk District Court.

≋ Angelita Sonoqui ≋

Court Records - Angelita Sonoqui
Tuesday March 2, 1909

734
Adultery

United States of America
vs
Jose M. Montoya and
Angelita Sonoqui

At this day comes J.L.B. Alexander Esq. United States Attorney who prosecutes the pleas of the government in this behalf and the said defendants are brought into Court and by E.B. Goodwin, Esq. their Attorney also comes, and thereupon this cause coming on for trial of the issues herein joined comes a jury impanelled as in a case of misdemeanor by consent as follows:

Rosel Cooley	John Green	F.E. White	D.A. Massie
J.M. Bryant	R.I. Troxell	W.A. Belles	Edw. T.Collings
G.D. Gordom	G.W. French	John L. Irvin	C.E. Hazelton

twelve good and lawful men and they are duly selected and tried, impanelled and sworn to well and truly try the matter at issue herein between the United States of America as plaintiff and Jose M. Montoya and Angelita Sonoqui as defendants, and a true verdict give accordingly to the law and the evidence.

And thereupon the indictment is read to the said jurors by the Clerk and the pleas of the said defendants thereto is made known to them, after which (Part may be missing) and the opening statement by the United States Attorney comes the evidence on behalf of the prosecution and M.A. Ivy, Geo. Kirkland are duly sworn and testify and Exhibit A is read in evidence by the United States Attorney, and Antilano Roblez, Maria Roblez, Maria Morales, Novatus Benzing and Joe Porterie are sworn and testify in behalf of the government, after which the United States Attorney rests his case and the defendants Montoya and Sonoqui are sworn and testify in their own behalf and C.W. Johnstone is sworn, at the conclusion of which comes the argument of the jury by the respective counsel and the said jury is instructed orally by the Court as to the law the instructions being taken down in shorthand by the Court reporter and a bailiff is sworn to take charge of the jury and jury retires to their jury room to consider their verdict herein, and the said defendants are remanded to the custody of the Marshal.

Court Records - Angelita Sonoqui

734
Adultery

United States of America
vs
Jose Montoya and
Angelita Sonoqui

At this day comes J.L.B. Alexander, Esq., United States Attorney who prosecutes the pleas of the Territory in this behalf and the defendants in person and by E.B. Goodwin, Esq., their attorney also comes; and thereupon the said jury is brought and upon being called by the Clerk and all answering to their names and being now present in the jury box return into Court their verdict in the above entitled action, which is by the Court ordered recorded by the Clerk and is in words as follows, to-wit: "United States of America, plaintiff, against Jose M. Montoya and Angelita Sonoqui, defendant, Verdict: We the jury, duly impanelled and sworn in the above entitled action, upon our oaths, do find the defendants guilty.

J.L. Irwin, Foreman"

and the said verdict being received and recorded by the clerk, is read to the jurors by the Clerk and they all replying that it is their verdict, it is accepted by the Court, and the said jurors are discharged from the further consideration of this case, and Thursday March 4th inst. At 9:30 a.m. is fixed as the time for passing sentence upon the said defendants in this case, and they are remanded to the custody of the Marshal.

At this day it is ordered by the Court that all the trial jurors lately impanelled in cases number 733 and 734 as well as all others in attendance be excused for the term.

Order to pay witness:

On this day came into Court, Elias F. Dunlevy, Clerk of said Court, and reported to the Court that he had examined under oath Ygnacio Estrada, a witness duly summoned to testify generally on behalf of defendant at the expense of the United States: that said witness is entitled to compensation, as follows, to wit:

Attendance March 2nd	One day at $3.00 per day	$3.00
	Total	$3.00

The Marshal is therefore ordered to pay said witness accordingly.

❦ Angelita Sonoqui ❦

CRIMINAL DOCKET

Docket 734
1908

(?) Nov. 16 Filed complaint, warrant, subp, final mittimus & certificate of proceedings

Min entry on return indictment
Filed indictment

17 Min. entry, each asked true name
Arraignment postponed till Dec. 18.

(?) Dec. 18 Min. entry, both defts arraigned & given till 1:30 to plead
Min. entry, Montoya pleads former acquittal former jeopardy and not guilty.
Min. entry, Sonoqui pleads former jeopardy and not guilty.
Bail each fixed 250 & set trial March 1.

1909
(?)27 Filed praecipe govnt wits.
Issued subp, Jesus Sonoqui, Maria Roblez, Antitano Robles, M.A. Ivy, C.W. Johnstone, & Geo. Kirkland.
6 copies subp

Mar. 1 Min entry contd for trial till March 2

2 Filed praecipe, issue subp Maria Morales govt wit 1 copy subp
Filed 2 subps. on return entered 2 orders each

Min entry trial to Jury & concluded

swg. 7 wits & interpreter for govnt swg. 1 deft. Jury list swg. 2 defts & 1 wit

Min entry on return verdict both guilty & fixing Mch. 4 at 9:30 for sentence.

Filed verdict

Mar. 4 Entered Judgment sentencing Montoya to 8 mos. In Terr Prison from Nov. 2

Entered Judgment sentencing Sonoqui to 4 months in Terr Prison from date.

Commitment for Montoya (Copy judgment with plaecita)
Certificate to copy seal to certif.
Commitment for Sonoqui (Copy judgment with placecita)
Certif to copy seal to certif

Docket fee (Trial to Jury).

☙ Frail Prisoners in Yuma Territorial Prison ☙

The Arizona Republican   December 18, 1908

U.S. GRAND JURY FINALLY ADJOURNED:
(In part)

Henry Lawson, Loretta Garcia, Jose Montoya and Angelita Sonoqui who had been indicted for a violation of the Edmunds act were brought before the court, but on their statements that they desired to be represented by counsel the matter of their arraignment went over until today.

Montoya especially did not want to make a move until he had consulted his attorney, "Missouri," the only name by which a large class of Mexicans know Judge E.B. Goodwin of Tempe.

December 19, 1908

The Trial of U.S. Cases All Go Over to March 1:
(In part)

On the United States side of the court Henry Lawson and Loretta Garcia were arraigned on an indictment charging them with a violation of the Edmunds act. They pleaded not guilty and their trials were set for March 1.

J. Montoya and Angelita Sonoqui, similarly charged, were brought in. Their attorney, E.B. Goodwin of Tempe, pleaded former jeopardy, saying that the defendants had been tried for this offense within the last three years. The plea at first excited some amusement but the evidence against the defendants is said to be the same that was used against them at the former trial, or else it is evidence strangely like it.

≈ Angelita Sonoqui ≈

TERRITORIAL PRISON AT YUMA, A.T.

Description of Convict

NAME:
  Mrs. Angelita Sonoqui
ALIAS:

CRIME:
  Adultery
COUNTY:
  Phoenix, Maricopa
LEGITIMATE OCCUPATION:
  Washwoman
HABITS:
  Temperate
OPIUM:
  No
HEIGHT:
  4' 11-1/2"
SIZE OF HEAD:
  6-1/4
COLOR EYES:
  Dark Brown
MARRIED:
  Yes
CAN READ:
  No
WHERE EDUCATED:

NUMBER:
  2942
SENTENCE:
  4 months from
  March 4, 1909
NATIVITY:
  Tucson, A.T.
AGE:
  29
TOBACCO:
  Yes
RELIGION:
  Catholic
SIZE FOOT:
  3-1/2
WEIGHT:
  100 lbs.
COLOR HAIR:
  Black
CHILDREN:
  No
CAN WRITE:
  No
FORMER IMPRISONMENT:

NEAREST RELATIVE:
  Mother - Ramona Cota

WHEN AND HOW DISCHARGED:
  July 3, 1909, Expiration of sentence

PRISON RECORD

Arizona Republican 12-18-08; 12-19-08
More description - Very dark; Forehead, low;
Teeth, good, Left incisor out.

Frail Prisoners in Yuma Territorial Prison

E.M. Bridgeford

Chapter 28

E.M. Bridgeford ~No. 3063

PRISON RECORD

Complexion - Fair   Forehead - Low   Carriage - erect

Bisbee Daily Review - June 9, 1909 (Court News)

In the case of the Territory vs. Mrs. E.M. Bridgeford, who was last evening found guilty of the crime of grand larceny by the jury which tried the case, an order was entered allowing the defendant to go on bond pending the hearing of a motion for a new trial.

July 1, 1909: Another was added to the number of those sentenced to Yuma in the District Court yesterday when Mrs. E.M. Bridgeford arrived here on the noon train and was sentenced in the afternoon on charge of burglarizing a house she had rented. She was given a two year sentence to serve and this afternoon left for Yuma accompanied by two dogs. Three other prisoners accompanied her and the jail is practically cleared of convicts.

TERRITORIAL PRISON AT YUMA, A.T.

Description of Convict

NAME:
  Mrs. E.M. Bridgeford
ALIAS:

NUMBER:
  3063
SENTENCE:
  2 yrs. from June 30, 1909

CRIME:
  Grand Larceny
COUNTY:
  Cochise
LEGITIMATE OCCUPATION:
  Lodging House
HABITS:
  Temperate
OPIUM:
  No
HEIGHT:
  5' 3-5/8"
SIZE OF HEAD:

COLOR EYES:
  Brown
MARRIED:
  Yes
CAN READ:
  Yes
WHERE EDUCATED:
  Illinois

NATIVITY:
  Illinois
AGE:
  40
TOBACCO:
  Yes
RELIGION:
  Protestant
SIZE FOOT:
  5
WEIGHT:
  121 lbs.
COLOR HAIR:
  Brown
CHILDREN:
  No
CAN WRITE:
  Yes
FORMER IMPRISONMENT:

NEAREST RELATIVE:
  Friend - Peter Cournaleen Bisbee, A.T.

WHEN AND HOW DISCHARGED
  Transferred to Florence
  Paroled by Governor Sloan September 7, 1910

~ Fannie King ~

Chapter 29

Fanny King~No. 3066

Daily Arizona Silver Belt   April 20, 1909

INDIAN WOMAN CUT TO DEATH IN QUARREL:
Drunken Quarrel Ends Fatally to
Mrs. Phoebe Hunt, An Apache

In a drunken quarrel over a young Indian, Mrs. Phoebe Hunt, an Apache Indian, was fatally stabbed Sunday night.

The wound was inflicted by a pocket knife. The blade penetrated the chest just above and to the right of the left breast, causing almost instant death.

Fannie, the wife of Guy King, is said to have committed the murder. Officers searched all day yesterday for her, but at a late hour last night, she had not been captured.

Jealousy is said to have been the cause of the murder.

It is stated on good authority that both squaws were infatuated with a young Indian by the name of Jacob Knight, known as Chile. In spite of the fact that both women were married, they both fell captive under the spell of the young buck's fascinations and under the influence of liquor, engaged in the quarrel which led to the death of Mrs. Hunt.

Soon after the murder, Fanny, Chile and Otto, a brother of the alleged murderess, disappeared. They are supposed to have gone together. Their disappearance heightens the belief that Chile was the indirect cause of the murder.

The husband of the murdered woman informed the sheriff's office of the killing, yesterday morning. He claimed that he did not see the murder committed, but that he left the women drinking in a pickup and in a few minutes was attracted by the screams of his wife. He claims that the King squaw did the stabbing.

The body of the dead woman was brought to the undertaking parlors of Jones & Son yesterday morning. A corner's jury was called during the afternoon and an examination made of the corpse.

Owing to the fact that there were no witnesses to be found, the inquest was postponed until 10 o'clock this morning.

It is expected that it will not be many hours before the suspected murderess will be in custody. It is not thought that she can escape, as a good description has been secured by the officers and she has had no chance to get very far out of the country.

Deputy Sheriff Duncan has been on the trail of the King squaw, with Undersheriff Frank Haynes assisting.

~ Fannie King ~

Fanny King~No. 3066

Daily Arizona Silver Belt   April 21, 1909

SQUAW ACCUSED OF MURDER LODGED IN PRISON:
Captured Near Rice Monday
Night by Deputy Sheriff Duncan

Mrs. Fannie King, an Apache squaw, charged with the murder of Mrs. George Hunt, another squaw, Sunday night, has been captured and is now in jail. According to the officers, the woman admits the killing.

She was captured Monday night on the Indian farm below Rice, by Deputy Sheriff Duncan. She was brought to this city yesterday afternoon and locked up, pending her examination.

The squaw was on the way to meet her husband, when she was arrested. She will receive no sympathy from him, as he declined to have anything to do with her when he heard of the crime of which she is accused.

To Deputy Duncan, the King squaw admitted killing Mrs. Hunt, but claimed that she did so after the dead woman had knocked her down and otherwise abused her. Her story is confirmed to a great extent by the evidence introduced at the coroner's inquest, yesterday morning.

At the inquest, the testimony was to the effect that two Indian boys, Otto Hunt and John Hopkins were fighting, when one of them threw a rock which hit Ben Norman, brother of Mrs. Hunt. The latter accused Fanny of being the cause of the fight and followed the accusation by striking her companion and knocking her down.

Fanny regained her feet in a few moments and, rushing at Mrs. Hunt, stabbed her with a pocket knife. The injured woman died a short time after.

The verdict of the jury was that the deceased, aged about 18 years came to her death from a knife wound inflicted by Fanny King. The jury was made up of Joe Windsor, George Rose, George Gamble, J.J. Dunn and A.J. Bennett.

The body of the dead woman was taken from the morgue yesterday by friends among her own race and buried with Apache ceremonies.

The King squaw will be given an examination in a few days.

☞ **Frail Prisoners in Yuma Territorial Prison** ☜

Daily Arizona Silver Belt   April 22, 1909

SLAYER OF INDIAN WOMAN BOUND TO GRAND JURY:
Remanded to Jail on Failure To Furnish
Required Bond For Appearance.

Fannie King, an Apache squaw, was held to answer before the grand jury on the charge of murdering Mrs. George Hunt, at the conclusion of her examination before Judge Hinson Thomas, yesterday.

Owing to the fact that the evidence showed that she had some provocation for the murderous assault, she was given the opportunity of securing her release by furnishing bail to the extent of $3,000. It is hardly likely that the woman can secure the necessary bail money.

Little new evidence was introduced at the examination. Fanny, through an interpreter, told of the killing, stating that she stabbed Mrs. Hunt after the latter had pulled her hair and knocked her down. Her bruised and bandaged face gave visual evidence in confirmation of her testimony.

The courtroom was crowded with Apaches and many more gathered outside the building and watched the proceedings through the windows.

The local missionaries are showing much interest in the case, as they have been working among the Apaches for some time, the husband of the murdered woman being one of their converts. It was at their request that she was given a Christian burial.

April 23, 1909

INDIANS DRAW SEVEN DAYS

For engaging in a fight which is said to have been the indirect cause of the murder of Mrs. George Hunt a few days ago, John Hopkins and Otto Hunt, both Apache Indians, were fined

～ Fannie King ～

$7 each in Judge Hinson Thomas' court yesterday. Neither man had the wherewithal to liquidate the fine and both were sent to jail.

June 29, 1909   SQUAW ON TRIAL: Fannie King, an Apache squaw, charged with the murder of Mrs. George Hunt, was placed on trial yesterday afternoon. The jury is as follows: J.C. McRae, F.D. Smith, Frank Ringgold, William Fisher, Bert Belluzi, E.F. Knowles, W.H. Childress, Thomas W. Bott, C.L. Baker, L.B. Doan, John Driscoll and R.R. Boyd. Jones & Flannigan represent the defendant.

The majority of the testimony will be heard today, as only the preliminaries were gone through with yesterday.
Fannie King

The Daily Silver Belt   **June 30, 1909**

FANNIE KING FOUND TO HAVE KILLED MRS. HUNT:
Mitigating Circumstances
Reduce Charges to Manslaughter.

Fannie King, an Apache squaw charged with the murder of Mrs. George Hunt, a member of the same tribe, was found guilty of manslaughter, yesterday afternoon.

While the evidence showed that Fanny had inflicted a knife wound on Mrs. Hunt, which caused the latter's death, it was also shown that there had been an altercation prior to the stabbing and that Mrs. Hunt had knocked Fannie down with a rock.

Under the circumstances, the jury brought in a verdict of manslaughter. The maximum sentence for a crime of this nature is ten years, but it is hardly probable that the squaw will receive the limit.

From the actions of the squaw yesterday afternoon, she did not even realize what was happening. While the jury was out and even after the verdict had been brought in, insuring her

Frail Prisoners in Yuma Territorial Prison

confinement in the territorial prison for at least a year, Fannie chatted gaily with members of her tribe, at the entrance of the sheriff's office.

Fannie will be sentenced this morning.

July 1, 1909: TWO YEARS FOR FANNIE KING:

Fannie King, convicted of manslaughter, as the result of her action in killing Mrs. George Hunt, was sentenced to two years in the territorial prison.

The fact that it was shown during the trial that Fannie acted in self-defense to a certain extent, entered into the action of Judge Lewis in giving her a light sentence.

She will probably be taken to Yuma later in the week.

July 3, 1909: SQUAW GOES TO PEN:

Fanny King, convicted of having killed Mrs. George Hunt, an Apache squaw, and sentenced to two years in the territorial prison, will be taken to the penitentiary at Yuma today by Eugene Shute.

Fanny King served 18 months of her 24 months term and was paroled by Governor Sloan on December 25, 1910. She was one of the three women transferred from Yuma to the new prison at Florence.

~ Fannie King ~

TERRITORIAL PRISON AT YUMA, A.T.

Description of Convict

NAME:
  Fannie King
NUMBER:
  3066
ALIAS:
SENTENCE:
  2 yrs from
  June 10, 1909
CRIME:
  Manslaughter
NATIVITY:
  Arizona (Tonto Apache)
COUNTY:
  Gila
AGE:
  19
LEGITIMATE OCCUPATION:
TOBACCO:
  Yes
HABITS:
  Temperate
RELIGION:
OPIUM: SIZE FOOT:
  No
  5
HEIGHT:
  5' 1-3/4"
WEIGHT:
  136 lbs.
SIZE OF HEAD:
COLOR HAIR:
  Black
COLOR EYES:
  Black
CHILDREN:
MARRIED:
  No
CAN WRITE:
  No
CAN READ:
  No
FORMER IMPRISONMENT:
WHERE EDUCATED:
NEAREST RELATIVE:
WHEN AND HOW DISCHARGED:
  Transferred to Florence. Paroled by
  Gov. Sloan December 25, 1910

PRISON RECORD

Listed under scars:
  over left eye, X on each cheek,
  on center of forehead,
  on nose & between the eyes,
  on chin, FANNY K with numerous small dots on back of right
hand - H T on back right wrist, HARRY, pin points, star and other Ink marks on back left hand.

Complexion - Olive   Forehead - Low   Carriage - erect
Teeth - Good

❦ Frail Prisoners in Yuma Territorial Prison ❦

Red Marie ❦ Ben Traywick

About the Author

The first Traywick to arrive in America was John, who landed in Charleston, South Carolina in 1662. He had two sons, John and James, the former eventually settling in Tennessee and the latter in Alabama.

Ben T. Traywick, a descendent of John Traywick, was born in Watertown, Tennessee on August 3, 1927.

James Joseph Wiggins, Ben's maternal great-grandfather, was a private in the Confederate Army, Company B, 16th Tennessee Infantry Regiment. Private Wiggins was killed in Perryville, Kentucky on October 8, 1862.

Benjamin Abbot Traywick, Ben's paternal great-grandfather, was a First Sergeant in the Confederate Army, Company G,-28th Infantry (2nd Mountain Regiment Tennessee Volunteers). Sergeant Traywick participated in all of the battles waged across Tennessee and Mississippi, from Chattanooga to Shiloh. At the end of the war, he resumed farming on acreage owned by the family.

Like his predecessors, Ben T. Traywick was military minded and enlisted in the U.S. Navy during World War II although he was only 15 years old, being tall for his age. Assigned to the U.S.S. Jenkins DD447 (Fletcher Class Torpedo Destroyer), attached to the amphibious forces in the Pacific, he had earned ten Battle Stars and a Presidential Citation by his eighteenth birthday. He served a second hitch in the Navy in the late 1940s, most of it in China. When the Communists overran China, he was on the last ship to evacuate Tsingtao. The remainder of his enlistment was spent on the battleship Missouri.

❦ Frail Prisoners in Yuma Territorial Prison ❦

Ben graduated from Tennessee Technological University with a B.S. Degree in Chemistry in 1953. After spending thirty years in exotic and high explosives in such places as Oak Ridge (Atomic); Sacramento (Missiles) and southeast Arizona (mining); he retired at the age of fifty-six.

Now he spends his time writing, researching Tombstone history, and visiting the far places in the American West and Mexico.

His first article was about a hillbilly sailor, called Saltwater McCoy. It was sold to "Our Navy" Magazine in 1957 and turned into a series. Ben has been frequently published in the Tombstone Epitaph since 1963. Since that beginning long ago, he has written more than six hundred newspaper and magazine articles. In addition, he has written forty-one pamphlets and books. His collection of "Earpiana" and Tombstone material is one of the best in existence anywhere.

Having been duly appointed by the Mayor and the City Council, Author Traywick is Tombstone's first and only City Historian to date. Ben and his wife, Red Marie, have lived in Tombstone since 1968. They have three children, Virginia Lynn, Mary Kate and William Maurice plus three Grandchildren; Benton Ivan, Rachel Marie and Joshua Cody. They are co-founders of the "Wild Bunch" and "Hell's Belles," now famous after twenty-two years in the O.K. Corral and one hundred sixteen films as of 1993.

Together, Ben and Marie have created the Tombstone Book Series, a number of volumes that depict the local history as it actually was. It is their wish that you will find these volumes both interesting, entertaining and enlightening even as they have experienced in writing them.